JAMES CALVIN SCHAAP

Sixty at Sixty

a boomer reflects on the psalms

D0681602

FAITH
ALIVE®
Christian Resources

Grand Rapids, Michigan

We welcome your comments. Call us at 1-800-333-8300 or e-mail us at *editors@faithaliveresources.org*.

Library of Congress Cataloging-in-Publication Data
   Schaap, James C., 1948-
   Sixty at sixty: a boomer reflects on the Psalms / James Calvin Schaap.
      p.   cm.
   ISBN 978-1-59255-440-9 (alk. paper)
   1. Bible. O.T. Psalms—Meditations. I. Title.
   BS1430.54.S33   2008
   242'.5—dc22

                                                                    2008020225

10 9 8 7 6 5 4 3 2

It's true I don't see him everywhere these days
but still, well, like this morning,
I was weeding the perennials,
dew-wet in morning glory light,
the wren singing his perky little heart out,
and suddenly, there was God again,
like a rabbit popping out of a strawberry patch,
God, just for a moment, taking my breath away.

—David Schelhaas

CONTENTS

Foreword by Eugene Peterson 7

1. He Knows 9
2. Commitment 11
3. Goose Bumps. 13
4. Hidden Faults 15
5. He Knows Our Days 17
6. Heritage 19
7. Mockers 21
8. Silence 23
9. God of My Righteousness. 25
10. Babes and Sucklings 27
11. Rejoice 29
12. Groaning. 31
13. Fretting. 33
14. Past Tense. 35
15. Each and Every One 37
16. Great Meek 39
17. In Season 41
18. Planted 43
19. All the Time 45
20. An Old Cat 47
21. Warning: Rewards 49
22. Wanting 51
23. The Legs of a Man 53
24. Restoration. 55
25. Waves and Breakers. 57
26. Forever. 59
27. Ordination 61

28.	The Keeper	63
29.	Remembrances	65
30.	Mercy	67
31.	Half-full	69
32.	The Ones That Run Our Lives	71
33.	Whose Sin Is Covered	73
34.	Be Exalted	75
35.	When?	77
36.	Those Who Take Refuge	79
37.	The Heathen	81
38.	When the Wicked Prosper	83
39.	Satisfaction	85
40.	My Glory	87
41.	Politics	89
42.	The Beauty of the Lord	91
43.	My Cup Overflows	93
44.	Surround Sound	95
45.	The House of the Lord	97
46.	Harmony	99
47.	Hallelujah	101
48.	Blessed	103
49.	Life and Death	105
50.	Wounds	107
51.	Perfect in Beauty	109
52.	Help	111
53.	Pilgrimage	113
54.	Wrath	115
55.	Understanding	117
56.	"Like a Day That Has Just Gone By"	119
57.	In His Feathers	121
58.	The Lord's Delight	123
59.	Bewonderment	125
60.	Heavenward	127

FOREWORD

Jim Schaap pauses on the cusp of sixty years of living, steps aside, and lets sixty fragments of old prayers often prayed, psalm phrases all, form six decades of people and experiences, conversations and observations, into a coherent story of faith. Sixty affords a good vantage point for remembering, gathering, and praying. Jim Schaap takes full advantage of sixty as he embeds sharply remembered shards of his life in a weathered mosaic of prayer, a mosaic bordered by the vast prairie landscape that is his workplace and home.

Psalm prayers have been doing this for those who pray them for three thousand years. The one hundred and fifty psalms at the center of our Bibles provide a personal center for praying everything that God reveals and everything that we experience in that revelation. They have been used this way for generation after generation of God's people, and there is no end to it. There seems to be nothing that men and women can experience that can't be prayed, and in the praying come to a deeper meaning than our emotions or circumstances or thinking can make of it.

The daily experience of living more often than not feels haphazard. It is one thing after another without apparent cause or consequence. We attempt to impose some order on life with a long-term plan or monthly calendar or daily schedule, but such devices are notoriously lax in keeping to the letter what is set down. Interruptions proliferate, accidents happen, appointments are missed, memories fail, anticipations fizzle. Storytellers train our imaginations in recognizing the possibilities of order in the seeming chaos, noticing relationships between people when they are not paying attention to one another, detecting the invisible connections that eventually accumulate into a plot.

Prayer is the deliberate, but also not infrequently spontaneous, attention we give to being open and responsive to the presence and actions of God in the making of our stories.

When the pray-er and the storyteller are the same person, as they are in these pages, we have a trustworthy companion as we make our way home along dangerously trafficked American roads.

American culture is not congenial to anything that cannot be measured or weighed, bought or sold. But the widespread consequence of this dismissal of the invisible is not happy. Boredom is epidemic; stress is lethal. Reared in such a world we have a difficult time realizing that we have any meaning or worth apart from the salaries or labels that others give us for what they see us do. So we are lonely because we so seldom have anyone pay attention to who we are as over against what we have done or pay for. False guilt seeps into our soul as we fail to meet the expectations of competence and self-reliance assumed to be normative in a "thingified" society. *Sixty at Sixty* is a timely antidote.

You don't have to be sixty. A pause at any age—thirty-two or forty-seven or seventy-five (my age)—in the storytelling and praying company of Jim Schaap is enough to recover a fading memory, revive sagging hope, or simply sink more attentively into what is going on with the people around us this day, and with what is going on with God, who is always with us.

Eugene H. Peterson
Professor Emeritus of Spiritual Theology
Regent College, Vancouver

1
HE KNOWS

"For the LORD watches over the way of the righteous."
—Psalm 1:6

I know one question and answer from the catechism I was raised with (I know more than one actually, but don't press me), and that is the very first—"What is your only comfort in life and in death?" The answer begins this way: "That I am not my own, but belong . . ."

One of the reasons this particular Q&A sticks to my otherwise Teflon memory is its tone and texture, its emotional color: the word of the moment here is *comfort*. What is your only *comfort*? What makes you feel good? What settles your nerves, helps you sleep, gets you over the blues?

The answer is, I am not my own. I belong to God.

Psalm 1's final verse begins with a phrase you can pull up to your chin on a cold winter night: "The LORD watches over the way of the righteous." But just for a moment, I'd rather consider the King James, which says, "He knows the way of the righteous."

God knows. God understands. It's no mystery to him. For the Lord God Almighty, right and wrong and good and ill are all part of a day's work. He knows. It's that simple, really. And that's immensely comforting.

Perhaps because life isn't. It may sound pessimistic, but when you add up the whole works, life amounts to nothing more or less than a sidewalk eighty years long, maybe, that leads to the grave. Not comforting!

My father died three years ago. I have the plaque he got after twenty-some faithful years at the bank where he worked. His employers ordered it from a place that turns out trophies for longest putt at company golf tournaments. On its own, that plaque is worth nothing. But it's on the bookshelf here in the basement because I just can't throw it away, even though the investment it represents is just gone.

Last week in church, a man stood up and asked for prayers for a woman in Chicago, half a continent away. She's dying of inoperable cancer, and her diagnosis is grim: she'll be gone in six months. I could have wept, honestly, even though I haven't seen the woman for years. I barely know her. As I grow older I am more affected by such stories. When I was young and the trajectory of my life seemingly had no end, I was nowhere near as affected by other people's miseries as I am today. Today other people's sadness weighs heavily.

Psalm 1 begins with a word that's hard to define—*blessed*—and it ends with a pretty strong hint at what "blessedness" means. In the tribulations that are ours—occasioned by sinners (like me) and by sin itself—we'll want to remember that God knows. God gets it. The Bible tells me so.

And it's not just a sweet idea. Be assured of it, says David, the shepherd poet. God knows the way of the righteous. God understands. His boy was once one of us, after all.

To be *blessed* is to know, in life and in death, in sickness and in health, that God knows—and loves—even us. That's blessed assurance.

Lord, "when sorrows come, they come not as spies, but in battalions." Sometimes these days, those sorrows and miseries seem greater and more frequent, and I feel so much less resilient. Hold me in your promises. I'm blessed to know that whatever I face—and whatever my neighbor faces— you know. Thanks for knowing. Amen.

COMMITMENT

"Commit your way to the LORD."
—Psalm 37:5

J ust had a look at the website of a couple of students I had in a writing class three or four years ago. I hadn't known that their nuptials were finally going to happen. The new husband sent one of those mass e-mails that directed family and friends to check out the wedding pix on their website. There were hundreds.

Both kids I liked, a lot. I really wanted them to get married, and, quite frankly, I think they lollygagged far too long. Like many twenty-somethings, they dawdled, finding it difficult, I suppose, to commit. I'm not sure what it is about their generation, but drawing a bead on the future—marriage, profession—seems a really arduous task for them. And it is, I guess.

No matter. I'm glad the two of them finally got married. I looked over some of the pictures—fairly typical stuff—a bunch of friends at the night-before barbeque and the rehearsal; then the wedding, some standard shots, many nice ones taken in the bride's family's orchard, rows of fruit trees running down from a family of smiling faces.

I wonder how this couple finally determined that this courtship of theirs—a good chunk of it carried on with a half a continent between them—was finally going to end in this ceremony. Maybe one of them said it was time to fish or cut bait.

Thirty years ago when my wife and I got married, it was easier to make commitments. Perhaps because the length and breadth of this world didn't seem as endless, the dangers as immediate, or the choices as wide. The world was smaller, more manageable; commitment didn't loom so ominously. And it's true that half of the wedding pictures people snap during this summer's round of nuptials will be burned within the next few years—or simply deleted. Lots of marriages fail. So this young couple had reason to pause, I suppose.

Commitments aren't easy for any of us. Yesterday's newspaper told of a local soccer star who had signed to play for one college after getting all sorts of ink for committing to a different one several months ago. So much for that *commitment*.

"Commit to the Lord," the verse says—buckle yourself in, sign on the dotted line, draw up a contract, become a part of something.

Commitments are daunting because nothing in our world today seems as precious as our freedom to choose. Commit to a college, and your choosing is behind you. Commit to a spouse, and you'll have to pick up your clothes *and* hang 'em in the closet. Commit to God, and what?

Commit to God and pack up all the *other* commitments and relationships—love of money, love of fame, love of power—and most of all, love of self. Commitment, an act of will, means giving yourself away. There are great rewards in committing to the Lord, but there's some cost too—yourself. The very essence of religious experience— you choose the faith—is the denial of self. Maybe that's why we balk so easily, kids especially, in this affluent age.

The road before my former students, now married, is straight and narrow. But love is worth it. Love is best.

I pray those wedding pictures will last.

Sometimes it seems we can't give enough to our commitments. Sometimes the need just doesn't end. And then again, there are moments—lots of them—when we couldn't think of being alone, when the very thought terrifies. Help us to commit and hold on to each other, and to you. Strengthen us for the journey. And be with those kids who've started a new life together. Amen.

GOOSE BUMPS

"Praise the LORD. How good it is to sing praises to our
God, how pleasant and fitting to praise him!"
—Psalm 147:1

I remember the goose bumps, my first. I was twelve maybe, part of a choir festival—hundreds of kids drawn from a dozen Christian schools—a half century ago in a small town in Wisconsin. The music was Bach—"Jesu, Joy of Man's Desiring." For almost fifty years I've not been able to hear that piece without remembering that day.

Those goose bumps appeared in an afternoon rehearsal before the big concert at night. I remember what that gymnasium looked like. I remember which step I occupied on the bleachers, and some of the kids around me. I remember being embarrassed because this unmanly tearful impulse—which I loved anyway—was still a threat that required testosterone to obstruct.

The music was gorgeous—you can't do much better than J. S. Bach. My girlfriend was there, and I haven't forgotten that either. She stood a row or two beneath me in the choir, and my seeing her there was part of the moment too. I don't know that the music alone would have raised such a visceral reaction. And I suppose faith was part of it—we were singing about Jesus, of course, and we were all kids from Christian schools. Being part of something so much bigger than myself had to play a role as well—all these kids were making a beautiful, joyful noise.

Psalm 147 says, first thing out of the box, how pleasant it is praise God—how *pleasant*. It's an amazingly human assertion: praising God simply feels good. The first declaration of this psalm has nothing to do with our duty ("we *should* praise him") or with God *wanting* our praise. Instead, the psalm starts with a statement that might appeal to the Me Generation: Hey, it feels good. And it's fitting too.

I wonder whether my skin turned inside out and my tear ducts threatened to spill over because, maybe for the first time, my "self" almost disappeared. That afternoon I got lost in the music, lost in affection, lost in the joyful affirmation of group love that is choral music, lost in all those things, lost in plain beauty, just flat-out lost.

Self-lessness is a good thing. Love is selfless. Heroism is selfless. Vivid spiritual experience is always selfless. When Mariane Pearl heard of her husband Danny's brutal execution at the hands of terrorists, she said she was able to handle it because she'd been chanting. She's Hindu. "The real benefit of having practiced and chanted was that at that moment I was so clear on what was going on. This is a time when I didn't think about myself at all," she says.

Sometimes it's just good to lose yourself. It's good to praise, to give yourself to God. It's good to love, to give yourself away. Praise — whether it's evoked by a Bach chorale or a bright new dawn — gives us a chance to empty ourselves.

That's good, I think, and it's pleasant. Best of all, our praise it fitting before the King — our King, the joy of man's desiring.

Thanks for goose bumps, Lord — thanks for the ability and opportunities to be thrilled. Thanks for letting us get lost in you, in the bounty of your beauty so evident in your world. Thank you that, once in a while, we can just disappear. Thank you for music, which does the job so well. Amen.

HIDDEN FAULTS

"Forgive my hidden faults."
—*Psalm 19:12*

Whenever I mow a certain patch of grass in my backyard, thirty feet west of our back door, a lingering memory comes back to me that will not die. What I feel when mowing the grass right there is a residue of shock, anger, envy, and pain. And the incident happened two decades ago.

When my daughter was in middle school, she was unceremoniously booted from the clique in which she'd been running. She cried for an entire day, nearly refused to go back to school, and wouldn't eat. Her father didn't understand. Her mother did—she'd once been a middle school girl.

Why that incident rises specter-like whenever I mow a certain section of backyard is Hitchcockian, I suppose; but what I feel at that moment—every summer weekend—is embarrassingly identifiable. It's anger and rage. Even though the mower is roaring, a certain junior high girl flashes her fangs from my memory, while her parents smile innocently. That's what I see. I'm fine once I get to the sidewalk.

My daughter, our oldest child, was suffering. Her father, himself a child as a parent, was only beginning to understand that about some things, he couldn't do a blasted thing. I hated both the kid and her parents, and that hate apparently found a place to settle permanently.

My daughter went on to high school, college, marriage, and a career, and now she is herself the mother of two beautiful kids. The girl who tossed her out is married with kids too. I don't hate her any more than I do our friends, themselves proud grandparents like us. But every time I mow a certain patch of grass—I swear it!—I get dragged back to a painful moment in my life as a father by a memory I don't even control. Makes no sense.

Not long ago I was visiting a classroom where students were required to read one of the stories I'd written. In preparation, I looked those stories over, not having read them for some time. What returned, as fully as my weekly mowing pain, was my state of mind when I wrote certain passages. No one else on the face of the earth would recognize what I felt, but reading those stories was like turning back the pages in an emotional journal mysteriously kept for me by my mind or my heart or my soul—I don't know which.

Maybe I'm going too far here. Maybe what David intends in this prayerful petition is simply for the Lord to clean out the sins David's not aware of, his sins of omission. We all have those—at least I do.

Whenever I become captive of some spooky part of my own subconscious, I can't help but be amazed at the sheer power of the human mind and spirit, and of the depth of our darkest memories. There's more going on than we are aware of, Horatio, even in our own minds and hearts.

Whatever's there, David begs, clean it up, Lord. Whatever I'm forgetting or missing or not acknowledging, make it shine. Forgive me. That's what's he's saying.

Protect us from injuries that have never really healed, Lord, the ones we're not even conscious of holding on to. Forgive us our sins, even the ones that don't haunt us, but are there living in some part of us. Create in us a clean heart, O God. Amen.

HE KNOWS  OUR DAYS

"The days of the blameless are known to the LORD. . . ."
—*Psalm 37:18, NIV*

I believe David—I honestly do. This isn't hyperbole or poetic license. I honestly believe him. But, like Job, I don't necessarily understand. Wish I did.

The joy of this line from David's song, its picture of open, warm, and loving hands extended to us each morning, is the assurance, simply stated, that God knows. God's not off on a cruise or so wrapped up with troubles in the Middle East that he has no time for our problems. The comfort of this verse is not only that God knows us—which isn't pocket change—but also that he knows our entire lives. God knows perfectly well what we live through each night and each day. That's what this verse says.

Those of us who suffer emotional or mental problems find life—simply living from day to day—an immensely severe trial all by itself. Those of us who care for them find ourselves dragged along, powerless sufferers too, of another stripe.

That famous Ecclesiastes passage doesn't say "there's a time to give thanks." If it did, maybe it would also suggest that there's also a time *not* to give thanks. And this morning is one of those times.

After a night of thick fog I'd rather not relive, I'm thankful for what my fingernails can find to hold. It would take so very little, it seems, for God to sneak some sunshine into the darkness, so very little. Believe me, time and time again I've asked the Lord to deliver the goods—day after day.

This morning's brilliant sunshine through the window above my head cannot brighten my heart and soul. But I am thankful for this single verse, even if it doesn't usher out the fog. Here's the promise that gives me morning breath: *God knows*.

I'm certainly not, by definition, blameless. Any psychologist would see quickly that I figure into the equation of emotional distress my loved one is suffering. But trust me, I'll take the promise any day of the week when the world looks as dark as it did last night—and again this morning.

God knows our days—all of them. The eternal God knows the times. He was here last night, and he's here this morning. Through some kind of divine physics, God constricts himself into the fleeting sweep of the second hand over every last clock I see. God's in my world. He knows. He's here.

Maybe something will change—maybe we'll take a step toward happiness, something ever so slight to push back the darkness, even if it's only for a couple hours.

Then again, maybe not. We've been on our knees so long I won't be surprised if nothing changes. And I'm not alone. I know dozens who suffer this way. But I believe that the poet and King is telling the truth: God knows every last one of our days.

That line of the angels to the shepherds—it's here again in this single line, in spades: Fear not. That's my comfort this dark morning—every morning, rain or shine.

Be thou my vision, Lord—see me through, as you have promised. Amen.

HERITAGE

"May your deeds be shown to your servants,
your splendor to their children."
—Psalm 90:16

I'm looking forward to a family reunion next week. I've been putting together a PowerPoint that features the family line, starting with the immigrants. I know the names of ancestors two centuries earlier in Holland, but no stories. The stories begin in the nineteenth century.

Great-Grandpa Hemkes must have been the quintessential absentminded professor. One Sabbath, before he came to America, he was so immersed in his theological meanderings that he nearly skated beyond the canals and out into the North Sea. His obituary suggests that, as a teacher, he was legendarily slack. Hmmm. I also read that people considered him a grand storyteller. He lived to be 82.

I find all of that somehow relevant, even useful.

His daughter, my Grandma Schaap, was an angel—and that reference comes from her in-laws. One characteristic of the Schaap family males is an almost unmanly sweetness, as if they're a bit short on testosterone. That gentle character likely came from her. Grandma Schaap, I'm told, was never particularly healthy, but then she had ten kids, a not immodest sum in those days, of course.

In Holland my Great-Grandpa Schaap was a seaman, a world traveler. But he tried to farm in America, like millions of other immigrants in the latter half of the nineteenth century. There was free land in South Dakota, where he lasted just two years. He left Holland because the small island where he'd lived didn't have a congregation of like-minded believers.

All of my ancestors were religious, very religious. They handed down a legacy of bedrock Christian belief in the Calvinist tradition.

But I'm sure some of those ancestors would wince if they'd read these pages. They carried convictions I don't have. They set stiff boundaries on Sabbath behavior and likely would have considered movies the lusty work of Satan. They never danced; and if they played cards, it was likely Rook, on the sly. They meted out their love for the Lord almost militarily and created communities by codes of austere righteousness.

Yet I'm their child in many ways. I have no doubt that part of the reason I'm writing these words is because of them and their faith.

I am not my father, just as my son is not his, even though he too has this predilection to believe. But he has, just as I have, this goodly heritage, which is sometimes more than a bit uptight. I want him to know that history and own that heritage, and to confess his faith in Jesus Christ too. I want him to believe, just as they, I'm sure, wanted me to, even though they'd immigrated to glory long, long before I—or my son—was born.

I know the impulse of this line from Psalm 90. Every Christian knows it. We want those we love to know the Lord. It's just that simple.

For those who don't show much of the goodly heritage of faith that flows in their veins, Lord, we pray. Help us not to rush to judgment. We all are led down our own paths. Thank you for the gift of believing parents. Bless us in our beliefs—and grace our ability to pass along what we so deeply treasure: your love. Amen.

MOCKERS

"Blessed are those who do not walk in step with the
wicked . . . or sit in the company of mockers."
—*Psalm 1:1*

The novelist John Gardner tells a story about his being the first to come on an accident—a long ways from anywhere. The driver, a woman, was alive but incapable of getting out of what was left of her pick-up.

The sad story he tells is not about the heroic efforts of the ambulance squad or the final dramatic moments of the woman's life. It's about himself. He can't forget his own pathetic realization, right then and there, that, for a moment at least, he found himself more interested in the details of the bloody scene—as material for his own writing—than he was in the woman's condition.

His heartlessness was a sin not of the flesh but of the head.

As a writer, I know that sin. But I also know it because I'm aging, and the older I become, the less "involved" I feel. I may feel more the pain of others' problems, but today I am far less driven by a sense of community than I once was. It seems clear to me that I'm needed far less than I once was.

And I'm simply less passionate. Today, what excites me more than principles is trying to understand why people choose them—and who does. I feel more and more like John Gardner at the scene of that accident, a bystander. Life is happening all around me, and I'm just fine on a La-Z-Boy. Maybe it's safer—who knows? I even walk more cautiously, afraid of falling.

But I know this too. Because it's easier for me to sit back and watch other people's windy passions, it's also far easier for me to ridicule them. Snipers never march; they hide. I'm an armchair quarterback who calls all the right plays.

I'd be more comfortable if Psalm 1:1 described the sinners we shouldn't hang around with as *scoundrels* rather than *scoffers*, or *murderers* rather than *mockers*. I mean, here in the small town where I live, fleeing the company of serial killers is not such hard work. Gangsters are, for me at least, far easier to avoid than scoffers—especially since I'm one of the latter myself.

I'm a college professor and a writer, and I'm getting old. That lethal combination—trumped by my own fallenness—makes scoffing far too easy, even in church, where it doesn't take much for me to ascend some lonely point on the wings of my own estimable wisdom and sneer at the silliness of others.

I wince to hear King David pick out scoffers and mockers as *most* unfit for the company of the righteous. Wish it weren't so. I rather like poking fun of other people and their silly passions. But maybe that's the point.

It's humbling to grow old, Lord, because it seems that in some ways we're no longer needed. Help me to take joy in others' work, others' contributions, others' joys and passions. Keep me from the easy cynicism of the easy chair. Help me to love as you have and to do as you do. Amen.

SILENCE

"Praise awaits you, our God, in Zion;
to you our vows will be fulfilled."
—*Psalm 65:1*

A country editor friend of mine, who unreservedly loves the small town in which he's always lived, once described to me how the great joy of his Sabbath began the moment he parked himself inside the church.

"I love my church," he told me. "I sometimes sit and look over my people there and my heart fills right up." It's the silence *before* the worship that he claimed to enjoy, the peace, the sense of being there with people he'd known for as long as he could remember, all of them quiet before the Lord. He loved those quiet short moments, he told me.

There's more to the story. You shouldn't think he sat down and immediately reached for the Kleenex. "But then," he said, "sometimes I dislike the whole business bad."

My friend's preferences remind me of that tireless optimist Ralph Waldo Emerson, who felt a related sensation once when he heard a preacher begin to hold forth, a preacher who "sorely tempted me to say I would go to church no more." Outside the church, says Emerson, snow was falling, a gorgeous spectacle. The preacher, however, was oblivious. "The snow storm was real, the preacher merely spectral," Emerson wrote, "and the eye felt the sad contrast in looking at him, and then out of the window behind him into the beautiful meteor of snow."

Exactly what David means with the first verse of Psalm 65 isn't clear, *awaits* being as good a choice as any for a Hebrew word whose literal translation, according to commentators, seems otherwise lost. The footnote suggests *befits* may be another possible translation. You choose. Either word offers a unique intent, or so it seems to me.

In *The Treasury of David*, Charles Spurgeon throws in some possibilities he's collected over the years and lists them with their sources: "God is most exalted with fewest words" (Alexander Carmichael); "Thy praise, O Lord, consists in silence" (Abraham Wright); "Praise without any tumult" (Andrew A. Bonar)—all of which make the country editor's blessed perceptions of an assembled, silent fellowship understandable.

People in our church are generously blessed and do wonderful things, often at the drop of a hat. But our Protestant story begins with a break from excessive formalism; and sometimes, to my mind, it tosses the baby out with the bathwater. There is no old-fashioned pre-worship silence in many of our churches because we chat, we fellowship. Silence, it seems, is overrated, hence banished.

I'd like to think that David knew what Thomas Carlyle did: "Under all speech there lies a silence that is better," he wrote. "Silence is deep as eternity."

When we take a rest from all of our words, we may well be camped in the neighborhood of David's real intent in this beautiful psalm's opening line, which I'd like to think begs us simply to "be still and know that I am God." Or something like that.

And now I'll stop talking.

⚒

Silence is a gift—at least to some of us. Help us to know when to speak and when to be silent. Give us the presence of mind and heart to be still in the circle of your love—not to crow but to cower. It's hard to yell when we're on our knees. Thank you for putting us there once in a while, Lord and Savior. Amen.

GOD OF MY RIGHTEOUSNESS

"Answer me when I call to you,
[O God of my righteousness]."
—Psalm 4:1

Charles Spurgeon says this particular descriptive phrase ("God of my righteousness") doesn't appear anywhere else in the Psalms, or in the entire Bible, for that matter. The King James version has it, as do plenty of contemporary translations, but the TNIV translates the phrase into a single adjective and then gives it to God ("righteous God"), a rendition that suggests a significantly different idea.

As I've said, I was born and reared in the Calvinist tradition, and I've stayed, for better or for worse—not always joyfully—within that fold. My Calvinism may be why I like the KJV's phrasing. Here the psalmist is giving full credit for his righteousness to the author thereof. I'm not interested in polemics, but he's doing the Calvinist thing.

I once knew a guy named Harry, perfectly bald, with only a quarter of a lung. He'd lost the rest to cancer, a smoker all his life. He was very much alone in the world. His wife was gone, but then she hadn't been at his side since he'd treated her the way he'd treated anything else in his life of real value—including his kids.

He wore a beret and drove an ancient VW beetle, looking for all the world like the eccentric he was. He loved to spin little aphoristic lines that rose in his mind and soul from all kinds of varied sources— some of them deeply devotional, some of them a bit randy, even sexy. Sort of like John Donne.

I'll never forget him crying, something he used to do at the drop of a beret. In a restaurant, outside church, inside church, just about anywhere, whenever he considered what he claimed to be the unrighteousness of his eighty-some years, he'd shed tears profusely— and he only had so much breath.

He'd look at me, a young man at the time, and raise a crooked finger. "Jim," he'd say, "if I had one thing, one lousy thing to do with my salvation, I'd burn in hell."

That had a way of ending conversation.

The poet in Psalm 4 is not pointing a crooked finger or trying to convince you and me to curb our appetites. Neither is he driven half-mad by the sins of his youth. I'm not sure he's crying at all.

But the intent of the line "God of my righteousness" is exactly the same as my old friend Harry's appraisal of his life's destiny. The psalmist is suggesting that without God the Father almighty, maker of heaven and earth, he'd register pretty much zilch on the righteousness meter.

It's difficult for me to understand how any believing person on this planet could say anything different. But then, I'm a Calvinist. At my age, looking back over a life that has some miles on it, I find it impossible not to say, *with* the poet of Psalm 4, and even with Harry, that this God I worship, this God who loves me, is, for certain, the "God of my righteousness."

⊰※⨯※⊱

If I had anything to do with my salvation, I don't know what it would be, Lord. I have absolutely no idea why you have blessed me with your love and favor — why I should be so graced. I don't know why, but I'll happily take it. Thank you. Amen.

10
BABES AND SUCKLINGS

"Out of the mouth of babes and sucklings
hast thou ordained strength. . . ."
—*Psalm 8:2, KJV*

It's amazing how much can be mined from a single line of words, especially when those words are considered the Word of God. When a book has been pored over by as many people for as many years as the Bible has, interpretations abound. So what exactly did David mean by verse 2, anyway?

First, a musical answer—a sound bite. Anyone who's ever watched a dozen kindergartners giving it all they've got on "Jesus Loves Me" knows something of what this verse intends. A bunch of kids can preach a sermon without once consulting a concordance—all they have to do is look earnest and sing out, and we all get blessed.

Art Linkletter made a career out a television show that's been off the air for decades—*Kids Say the Darndest Things*. And Bill Cosby made millions smile simply by chatting with five-year-olds. You know why kids are so compelling—ask any available grandparent, and you'll get a half-dozen stories recounting the insightful off-the-cuff comments of ordinary preschoolers.

Surely there's some of that in this psalm verse.

Christ himself more than occasionally admonished his followers that, when it came to faith, we should all be like kids—simple, uncritical, accepting. Childlike faith has to be somewhere at the heart of David's intent too.

John Calvin thought there was something else at work here in this line—an appreciation of the miracle of life as we receive it from the hand of the Creator. Calvin wanted us to notice that babies, the moment they are born, are already sucking; without being taught, they are already doing the only thing they need to do in order to get the one thing they need, breast milk. Another miracle. In the broadest sense, that is *providence*. And that, Calvin claimed, is simply miraculous. A nursing child is proof of a loving God, a Creator/Father of incredible magnificence, power, and love.

Sounds right.

Yesterday in church, a woman stood up before we prayed and told us that her granddaughter, her only grandchild, had been taken off the continuous IV she'd been on since being born six weeks premature at just two pounds. She was not much more than a handful of precarious life. This darling child, the woman said, was now way up to three pounds, and—can you believe it?—taking a bottle for the first time.

David, the poet king, had no notion of the United States, nor of a little prairie place called Sioux County, Iowa. He could not have imagined the church we worshiped in yesterday or the clothes we wore. He would have been astounded by the child's life—that beloved granddaughter wouldn't be alive if we were Israel, B.C.

But when that young grandma boldly announced her joy to the rest of us, I knew that she understood Psalm 8:2 in a way entirely her own: "Through the praise of children and infants you have established a stronghold."

Yesterday in our church, no one understood what that verse means better than she did. I'm sure of it.

Thank you for children. Thank you for the sense of renewed life we take from their antics. Children make every day the first day of spring. Bless our kids and our grandkids. Bless them with your love, and show them your face. Amen.

11
REJOICE

"Rejoice in the LORD and be glad, you righteous. . . ."
—Psalm 32:11

All day yesterday, intermittent screeches came crashing through the open basement window of my office. A son of the couple who used to live next door was cleaning out the junk—old tools, two by fours—from his deceased father's three-stall garage, creating a sprawling pyramid that attracts me for some shady reason. But I'll do my best to stay away.

I couldn't see the guy from where I was sitting, but I heard every last armful of trash come down on the pile every time he emerged from the shadowy interior. His father was an ace tinkerer and a packrat, so the son's job was colossal.

The pile of stuff one accumulates throughout life is incredible. Sometimes I think I'd like to move out of town where the massive prairie sky is a daily—and nightly—art museum. What keeps me from looking for another place, however, is the gargantuan task of moving, which would necessarily include the job my neighbor's son was doing yesterday—throwing out mountains of really valuable stuff. I just couldn't do it.

Here in my office, I'm surrounded by things I couldn't think of tossing, things that will, someday, be just so much crap to my kids. Maybe I ought to buy one of those little guns that produce plastic labels: "This is a trophy I got for longest putt at a teachers' tournament in Lafayette County, Wisconsin." I'm sure my son would want to keep it.

Upstairs, I've got two shelves of old Dutch books, some of which came from my grandfather and great-grandfather, preachers in the olden days. There are others, a dozen at least, that I bought for almost nothing at an auction. Some of them were published about the time the *Mayflower* dropped anchor off Massachusetts. When I'm gone, will anyone care? Or will those ancient texts simply be returned to another auction, where some anxious fancier will pick them up for peanuts and put them carefully on another bookshelf until she dies, in an endless cycle?

That junk pile next door reminds me all too clearly of my own life's detritus, a thought that would never have entered my mind twenty years ago but now is painful and haunting.

By human standards, it's impossible to deny that life is tragic—there's no escaping the grim reaper, after all. Life is like licking honey from a thorn, someone told me recently. Everyone must die. Count on it. All things must pass. Someday, my books, my baseball trophies, my ergonomic keyboard—it's all got to go. Even my wife, my children—and theirs, my beloved grandkids, we all will die.

Like so many Bible verses, for those of us steeped in them, the last verse of Psalm 32 barely makes a sound in the ongoing din of my overextended life. It's altogether too easy to pass over. "Rejoice," says the forgiven King David. "Rejoice in the Lord and be glad." It's not a whimper or a whisper. It's a shout, because what needs to be routed is the despair we all inherit as flesh weakens and spirits collapse before a rectangular hole in the ground.

Rejoice, David says. Rejoice and be glad. Rejoice in God's love because the Lord, the almighty tinkerer, makes all things new, even the junk next door—the pile here in my office and the mess in my heart.

Rejoice and be glad because God our Savior never tosses a thing he loves.

⌇⌁⌇✕⌁⌇

*Until we look around at our own messy lives, it's so easy
to think it's the guy next door who's storing up all his
treasures. We've all got those piles, Lord—far too much.
Even if we've never worshiped the almighty dollar, we've got
dross that just won't quit. Help us to see our lives as a portal
to eternal life in your presence. Amen.*

GROANING

"I remembered you, God, and I groaned;
I meditated, and my spirit grew faint."
—Psalm 77:3

There are times when I nearly lose my wife in church. Maybe I should say she nearly loses herself. Maybe we attend too often—twice every Sunday. Maybe we've attended for too long, both of us—entire lifetimes. Maybe it's the congregation—a wonderful place full of many, many happy faces. I don't know the reasons, but yesterday in church, both times, I nearly lost her. She doesn't sing, doesn't read along, doesn't seem to be into it at all. At the end of the sermon last night, she was looking down at her hands, and had been for a long, long time.

She is my wife, and I believe I understand her, although with each passing year I'm less sure of our being able to enter the corners of each other's individual secret places. But I know something of what she is feeling because I feel it too.

This entire weekend has been one of those that both of us hope never, ever to experience again. "No young man thinks he shall ever die," Hazlitt once wrote, in one of my all-time favorite aphorisms. But neither does any young man believe he will become the father of adult children. Trying to make it though your child's suffering—your adult child's suffering—is nothing you can prepare for. It's a black hole that threatens to engorge everything.

It is the lot of parents to worry even more than their children, I think—even when those children create the worry, and even when they themselves worry. I don't live in my son's skin; I don't know what he's feeling from moment to moment. So what I'm left with is the deadly sting of those few moments when I *do* know, moments when what I see in him is poison. He may well go back to his apartment, turn on some music, or watch a flick, and walk right out of the darkness.

Not so, us. We spend the rest of the weekend in a midnight winter.

Our kids' problems inflict wounds whose bleeding doesn't stanch easily. Blood spatters all over. It smears the walls in the living room and pools in the bedroom. And when we go to church, we track it right into the pew.

That's why I say I almost lost my wife yesterday in church.

Honestly, I know of no better way to understand what Asaph is talking about here in Psalm 77. In the night, with his hands extended, Asaph hoped and prayed for blessing that flat-out didn't come. What he remembers is the very language of his groaning. Because he's known better times, the absence of blessing, when all the world seems aligned against him, triggers spiritual, mental, and even physical pain that is excruciating.

Sometimes our cries and prayers, like Asaph's, seem to fall on stone-deaf ears. That realization is the peculiar pain *only* of those who know God. When our Lord doesn't pick up the phone, believers feel unspeakably alone, even in worship. Maybe most alarmingly then.

"I remembered you, God, and I groaned."

Been there, done that.

Today, even if you don't answer a single one of my petitions, Lord, please give an ear to someone who thinks you're not listening. Fill him or her with your Spirit. I know what it's like to feel as if no one is home, and there are tons of folks who feel that way right now. You're there, and I know it. Thank you for bringing me through the deep waters. Amen.

13
FRETTING

"Do not fret because of those who are evil
or be envious of those who do wrong. . . ."
—*Psalm 37:1*

y mother, who is gloriously upbeat in many ways, tells me she thinks the world is sinking toward some iniquitous black hole that will suck most of us in until the Lord, in glory, comes again. She frets about our culture's seamy edges, and her continual fretting affects her mood. She listens to too many radio talk show hosts.

She's old enough to deserve my respect no matter what her views or how much she frets. Besides, she's my mother. But I wish she wouldn't spend the last years of her life fretting the way she does.

We live in strange times. I can't think of an era in the last century when spirituality was quite so popular. Most Americans claim to believe in God. A significant majority attend worship frequently. Crime is down, as is drug use and teen pregnancy. Even abortion rates are lower than they were.

Just about every college student at the school where I teach wears a T-shirt with a Bible verse. Students flock to praise &worship gatherings voluntarily and exude a piety that existed only among the most devout kids just twenty years ago. Lots of parents tell me their kids are far more spiritually mature at eighteen than they were at that age. Most of them go on church mission trips or work groups, many of them to the poorest regions of the world. Where I live, faith is almost hip.

For the last few years, the United States government has been in the hands of Republicans, my mother's party. Many politicos and pundits claim the 2004 presidential election was a wake-up call to opinion leaders who never took Christians seriously. Most major newspapers now concede that for too long they didn't have a clue about evangelicals—a huge segment of the populace. Today it's not hard to find stories about faith in your local newspaper or on the news.

It's difficult to argue that we're all going to hell in a hand basket, although Mom sure thinks so. What troubles her is that this nation is becoming secular, forbidding prayer and tolerating abortion, tossing the Ten Commandments.

I think she's fretting way too much. She thinks I'm even worse off—a liberal.

In the world where I live, wind storms called "dusters" got so thick and black in the thirties that people were killed. When a big one blew up in Oklahoma or Kansas or western Nebraska, when it got really dark in the middle of the day and wet blankets or sealed windows couldn't keep dirt out of the house, good Christians thought it was the end of the world.

A host of believers I know plot out the trajectory of our time in the same direction—things just keep getting worse and worse and worse. . . .

Maybe I don't fret enough. Maybe I'll start in a few years. Maybe it's another sign of aging.

Meanwhile, both Mom and I can take heart from verse 1 of Psalm 37, which says, in a nutshell, "Don't fret." The enemies—whoever they are—aren't worth my time or anxiety, nor are they worth hers.

Next week, maybe I'll quote that verse when I see my mother. Maybe it will help!

⊰⊱✕⊰⊱

Free me from the desolation of desperation, Lord. People around me who are getting older seem to grow more pessimistic. Give me courage to face a world that's ever tougher to understand. Give me grace for the journey, especially when I've turned the corner and am coming down the homeward way. Amen.

PAST TENSE

"I cried out to God for help; I cried out to God to hear me."
—Psalm 77:1

The kid was eighteen, in his last year of high school, the last month and a half, really. He was on his way to the state high school basketball tournament.

It was one of those accidents that could have happened a hundred miles away but didn't. It happened on a nondescript intersection people have crossed for years on their way to work and never noticed, an intersection minutes from home. Three guys had just started a little trip to the state capital, and just like that, one of them was dead.

I'm glad I'm not the law, because what kind of penalty could you exact that would be worse than what's already happened? The guy is dead. Someone who, by all accounts, was a great kid. Someone who, just days ago, had professed his faith in God. For causing that, someone else already has a life sentence.

The poet of Psalm 77 starts with history, repeated like a mantra. "Here are the facts, Lord. In the past, when I cried out to you for help, you answered. That's what I know of your love. You were there when I needed you. My cries were never bootless, never empty."

One of the reasons the shocking, accidental death of a kid a couple hundred miles away from the chair where I'm sitting is so frightful is that his friends likely have no such history. Unlike the psalmist, kids generally can't recite chapter and verse of earlier distress or horror. The sudden, inexplicable end of a life is shockingly new.

Yesterday a friend of mine held forth in chapel about the scriptural phrase "not a hair can fall from your head." He did a careful analysis of every such simile in the Bible and showed forcefully and convincingly that the phrase itself is scriptural shorthand for life itself. He referred to specific tragedies suffered recently in the community, even mentioning the loss of his own son years ago, and then passionately offered this eternal bromide: God himself will never leave us, even in death.

At just about the same time he was speaking, some very tragic news was hitting a rural community in Minnesota—one of their own, a really good kid, was dead.

I never knew that young man. He'd decided to come to the college where I teach next year, but somewhere in a campus office this morning, his application will be filed elsewhere. If years were moments—and in an eternal way they are—he might have been in chapel yesterday to hear the powerful lesson about hairs falling.

The apostle Paul says in Romans 5 that suffering builds perseverance, perseverance builds character, and character creates hope. It sounds good at a distance or in a rearview mirror. Makes great sense if we've got a history.

In rural Minnesota this morning, hundreds of people are crying, many of them kids. They're losing some innocence and gaining a history. Maybe someday the words of the psalmist will be theirs too: When I bawled, you wiped my tears—remember? But this morning they're learning.

May the God of peace answer them, just as he answered the chapel speaker, as he's answered me, as he answered the psalmist. Past tense.

Be there, God. That's all the poet asks. And it's enough.

⚹

Only those who've already suffered know the beat of this line, Lord, because we know that it's true—you've been beside us in awful suffering. This morning, those kids in Minnesota and other people all over the world are learning. Be there, as you promised, as you have been. Amen.

15
EACH AND EVERY ONE

"He determines the number of the stars
and calls them each by name."
—Psalm 147:4

Yesterday, as I was walking up the grand stairway at the college where I teach, some kid came racing out of the offices upstairs and literally flew right past me, down the stairs and out the door, his feet a blur. The way he took that staircase on was a show, I swear, incredibly artful.

I stood there, halfway up, and remembered not only that once upon a time I could do that too, but also that I can't anymore. I stood there stunned, realizing that I felt the way my grandpa must have once felt. Now my grandpa is long gone, and I am him.

I have a cold, and it's nothing to shake a hanky at. It started way down in my lungs about a week ago, fetching a cough I've been battling since. Yesterday, enemy forces climbed up my windpipe and took my sinuses hostage. This morning I awoke with a mouthful of fine, dry sand.

We haven't heard from our son in more than a week. We hope he's doing well, all alone so far away. We pray he'll find some friends, folks with whom he can be at home. We want him in church. We're not sure of much, and haven't been for several years.

This, my thirty-sixth year of teaching, hasn't started out with joy. For the first time in all those years, I believe I'd move if the right opportunity were to come up. But who on earth would invest in someone who's barely going to get into the parking lot before leaving for retirement? Makes me feel dismal.

I'm facing a ton of student papers I have yet to read. I've had them far too long. My students have every right to roll their eyes when I come into class without them.

My wife's cholesterol spiked. She never knew she had a problem until the good doctor called a few weeks ago after reading her test. "You better start some pills," he told her, and wrote out the prescription. She's been on them since.

Her mother's life is precarious, and in many ways she'd rather be gone. She's not morbid about it, nor deeply depressed, but has little sense of her own use on this wintering earth. She thinks she's a burden. Last week there was a bout with an ambulance. She vows, never again.

There are probably more laments around me if I set out to listen to the dark voices.

To imagine that God knows that whole laundry list is beyond belief. To believe that same God loves me, despite my curmudgeonliness, my insistent listing of my own problems as first and foremost in the universe, is absurd. To imagine that somewhere in that all-knowing mind the Lord has drawn a divine bead on me is incomprehensible — not only because of the long list of my own ills but even more because of the billions of "me"s who populate this world of his.

Out here in the country, I see the night sky better than most city-dwellers. I know the stars above are countless. The comfort of Psalm 147:4 is that God knows them all, every one. God knows what's happening in their air space, he "calls them each by name." That's our great joy.

And he knows our aches and pains — every one of them. That's why by faith I know I'm not just baying at the moon or whistling in the dark.

<hr />

Lord, countless people in your world have it worse than we do. In a half-minute we could name a dozen caught up in wars, murders, accidents, cancer, or lifelong suffering. How some people cope is beyond me. Even though my sniffles don't rate, comfort me with the assurance that you know. Bless me with the conviction of your promises. Nothing is greater than the medication of your unfailing love. Thank you. Amen.

16
GREAT MEEK

"But the meek will inherit the land and enjoy peace...."
—Psalm 37:11

By the standards of traditional orthodoxy, Christian piety is never good enough. "Give all that you have to the poor and follow me," Jesus told a rich young CEO. The guy, Harvard-trained, returned to his office desk.

The injunction to righteousness can be crippling because even a heartfelt desire to do good is, in plain fact, never good enough, as Martin Luther observed, his knees bloodied. We're saved by grace, not works, and the combined good deeds of all the Boy Scouts on the planet won't make a difference. That's what the good book says.

I find lines like Psalm 37:11 disconcerting. It declares the glories of a piety that's unattainable. Maybe it's all the fault of my Aunt Meek.

Physically, she was, like most of the Schaaps, small and square. Like most of my father's brothers and sisters, she had an adolescent giggle—a little warble that eventually rose into an off-key falsetto, so that sitting in a room of Schaaps was like being surrounded by seagulls. Her name was Marie, but everyone called her "Meek." As a child, I knew her before I knew the biblical word, so I thought of her as it.

My father's family was all good, good people. A cousin told me that a marriage counselor once said her problems were caused by having a father—my uncle—who was "too good." What a blessing!

Aunt Meek's children—themselves retired today—could likely recount moments when she fumed or flashed hot bolts of anger. She could not have always been as soft and gentle as I knew her. Even so, humble, kind, and sweet, she had to be among the kindest of human souls. Having Aunt Meek as the model for biblical *meek* makes me feel crippled by a standard I can never reach.

Not long ago, frustrated by the honchos at work, I stood up in a faculty meeting and accused them of lack of leadership. Some lauded the speech; others disliked it a ton. But what's clear to me is that I wasn't acting like Aunt Meek. I was abrasive and, some might judge, more than a little arrogant in my desire to slap up my superiors.

When it comes to inheriting the land, I'm out of the will.

Will peace be the blessing only of those who don't rock the boat? Does servanthood imply servility? I know this much: that speech of mine did not grant me peace. I spent sleepless nights wondering if I'd said too much, gone too far.

If rising temperatures and volcanic behavior is created by pride — *my* desire, *my* will, *my* personal sense of injury — then I'll be a renter and never inherit God's bountiful blessings.

Here's the $64,000 question: was it wrong for me to speak up as I did in that meeting? That's for me to determine, prayerfully, and, I guess, meekly. Strange as it may seem, it has to be possible to fight injustice meekly. That's not oxymoronic. It can't be. The Bible tells me so.

Pride, however, always goeth before the fall. That truth I need to bring home into my heart, meekly.

———— ✕ ————

I know it's not always wrong to speak up, Lord. To be meek doesn't mean acting like road kill. Grant me a whole heart and a large soul to distinguish motives, to separate self-interest from righteous judgment, to know when I should speak up — and when I'm simply venting. Forgive me when I'm wrong. You know it happens too often. In Jesus' name, grant me my petitions. Amen.

17
IN SEASON

"... which yields its fruit in season ..."
—*Psalm 1:3*

I t only takes a phrase from Ecclesiastes 3 ("For everything there is a season. . .") for my mind to spin an old record by The Byrds, a late sixties rock group, and I hear those famous verses set to the music of Pete Seeger's tune "Turn, Turn, Turn."

Correction. Maybe I should say my *heart* plays that tune, because the energy that spins that vinyl originates deeper in my psyche than my mind. My heart remembers; my heart weds "Turn, Turn, Turn" to flower children and the antiwar movement. In a second, I feel a joyful, lilting nostalgia—*my* music, *my* history, *my* past. Peace signs, bellbottoms, and flower power—the whole era. Free at last, thank God almighty.

That particular song continues to thrill me, I think, because in the tight Christian world of my teenage years, "Turn, Turn, Turn" was the closest thing I knew to a hymn from the music of my world. It was a biblical text, after all, and therefore reminded the rebel in me that the Bible itself says there's a time for war *and* a time for peace.

And maybe this is a time for peace, I told my parents, who were hawks, back then. *You're wrong about rock music, wrong about Nixon, wrong about Vietnam.*

That's where the conversation ended, time and time again, and I'd go up to my room, turn up the volume, and play that song once more.

I still get goose bumps from "Turn, Turn, Turn."

But I'm older now, and I understand there's more to those verses in Ecclesiastes. That memorable chapter isn't just hippie doctrine; it's not just the Bible's own manifesto that everything is legitimate—

how did that other song go?—everything is beautiful in its own way. Ecclesiastes is countercultural all right, but it's not just for bellbottoms.

This single clause from Psalm 1:3 is a reminder that, sure, everything is legit, but *only* within its time. "There is a season," after all, just as there is *not* a season. There's good timing and there's bad timing.

That man or woman who is blessed, the poet king says here, will—and you can count on this—yield fruit *in season*—which is to say, *at the right time,* the right time to bear exactly the kind of fruit he or she should bear. Back then, I don't think I was ever arguing for propriety—more like "fruit basket upset."

Order is blessed, it seems, according to Ecclesiastes 3 and Psalm 1. Chaos is anathema; even though when I say that, in the context of the late sixties, I sound as schoolmarmish as my parents did to me. Maybe it's worth noting that the Byrds's only other hit was "Eight Miles High," a celebration of hallucinogenic drug use.

But then again, maybe what the Bible says about propriety here resonates more in the mind and heart of a man as old as I am, someone who, several years ago already, began to really like staying home at night. Maybe "blessedness as order" is as comfortable as bedroom slippers to a man who looks forward to the long breath he takes when those darling grandchildren finally go home.

For everything, after all, there is a season.

But that old album is here somewhere yet. I really ought to spin it again. It's a joy. And there's a time for that too.

Sometimes I'm not sure what to do with my own memories, Lord. I'm surprised at what I remember and what brings joy. I'm thankful for memory, thankful for that bank of oldies—the music, the stories, the perceptions. I'm thankful for a good, good life. Thank you for being there, always. Amen.

PLANTED

"... like a tree planted by streams of water..."
—Psalm 1:3

Once upon a time, my father received a job offer from an association of Christian schools in another state. I don't remember the offer myself because I was far too young, but I know my father well enough to imagine how thrilled he must have been—to him, working for Christian education would have been like being in the direct employ of the Lord God almighty.

At the time, he was doing accounting work for a heavy-equipment industry run by a bunch of yahoos who liked to wheel and deal and party far better than my father, the preacher's kid.

Armed with that blessed new job offer, he must have gone the rounds. I'm not sure what my mother said when he told her. But I do know what happened when he spoke to my grandfather, his father-in-law. Grandpa cried. My father told me that, years later.

Grandpa cried because he didn't want his daughter to move so far from his new home, a block away from the heart of the village where his blacksmith shop/gas station stood. Grandpa cried because he didn't want his grandchildren gone. Grandpa, the blacksmith, bawled, and Dad hung in for a few more years with the heavy-equipment roisters.

There's always more to the story, and this one has some significant antecedent action. Grandpa's only other daughter was killed in a freakish car accident not that many years before. Grandpa—and Grandma—had already suffered the death of a child. They didn't want to lose another, even if only by distance.

I'm told that my grandfather's emotions were legendarily promiscuous. But I never lost a child, and he did. So if he bawled when my father told him about a job offer that my father might have believed came directly from the Lord, I'll forgive Grandpa.

Most fiction begins in the mind of the writer with a single question: what if? What if my aunt hadn't been killed and my grandpa hadn't cried? Would my father have left the state and taken the job of his dreams? And if that had happened, what if I had grown up in a whole different world?

Who on earth would I be?

So it's of more than passing interest to me that the tree of Psalm 1 is "planted." Someone put it down on the banks of that metaphorical river. The particular spot wasn't necessarily the choice of the whirligig maple seed; that spot was chosen.

When I think of the blacksmith's tears, it's almost impossible to believe that we are not our own. But there must be a design to this madness. Someone's in control. Someone, or so it seems to me, does the planting. I'm a witness.

<hr />

The mystery of our lives—our fortunes, our places in this world—is almost beyond us. Who are we, Lord, but your creatures, the work of your hands, your own blessed handiwork? Thank you for that knowledge, a comfort each day but especially when we fear the unforeseen. Stay with us. We know you will. Amen.

ALL THE TIME

"Day after day they pour forth speech;
night after night they display knowledge."
—Psalm 19:2

I n Psalm 19, and in this verse particularly, David is not given to hyperbole or flashing his poetic license. What he's established in the opening verse is that God himself is "proclaimed" in the expansive beauty of the heavens. A prairie landscape is the voice of God, he says, and that voice is there *all the time*, day after day and night after night. It's music that never stops, a celebration as eternal as anything this world can deliver. And it all speaks of God. Isn't it glorious? That's what David is saying.

What makes him hammer the point home in verse 2 may well be that he can't seem to believe it himself. Literally, God almighty has created a canopy of praise that soars above us *all the time*. "Day after day," he says, as if he just can't take it all in. "Night after night," he continues, in case we're not paying attention. Stop your infernal toiling and spinning once in a while, he says, and look up, for heaven's sake.

In her essay "Gypsies," Anne Lamott, in her own inimitable fashion, ridicules herself for being so infernally self-obsessed. If she hasn't already arrived, she's dreadfully close to middle age, she says, and, when she sees herself in a mirror, she finds the telltale marks — "triangles of fat that pooch at the top of my thighs" — terrifying.

Some of her friends ask her to come along to a movie about gypsies, and she does, albeit reluctantly, because she's angry about her own aging body. She would have preferred "an action movie, something with some tasteful violence."

But the movie they attend brings her joy because it shows old women dancing with a level of measured self-abandon that she knows she needs. What she sees in their eyes is a portrait of the equanimity that promises, if we let it, "the beauty of having come through." Honestly, some of us long ago stopped fearing class reunions.

For Ms. Lamott, the movie she watched was, like the heavens, the very voice of God. What she sees is exactly what she needs—not to cover her wrinkles but to bless them. Those old dancing women remind her that she, like them, is becoming sanctified. They make her crow's feet smile.

> Coming out of the movie that night, I realized that I want what the crones have: time for all those long, deep breaths, time to watch more closely, time to learn to enjoy what I've always been afraid of—the sag and the invisibility, the ease of understanding that life is not about doing.

David the poet-king would resonate with those words, I think. The everydayness of God's voice above us is so startling only because we *don't* pay attention, because *I* don't pay attention. Like Lamott, I'm still acting as though life is more about doing than about being, more about proving myself and getting things done than about simply watching the sky.

The heavens are declaring right now, David says, this very instant, and they're not about to quit. We only need to stop, and look, and listen. Day after day after day.

⁂

Maybe I still work too hard, Lord, but I'm learning. Slowly but surely, I'm learning to smell the roses. Maybe it's one new joy for all the slaps old age brings. Sometimes I wonder how many sunsets I've missed. Help me get out there and look, day after day, and thanks for the heavenly preaching. Amen.

AN OLD CAT

"... The earth is full of your creatures.
There is the sea, vast and spacious, teeming with
creatures beyond number — living things both large and
small. There the ships go to and fro, and the leviathan,
which you formed to frolic there. All creatures look to you
to give them their food at the proper time."
—Psalm 104:24-27

The highest I ever got on my summer job during college was about five feet off the ground aboard an old war-surplus Caterpillar. I'm not sure why the boss made me the designated driver, but he did. So most days I sat at the hand levers that controlled the old beast, an ancient, faded yellow wonder whose huge engine banged, banged, banged along the beach as if it had but one mammoth cylinder.

Four or five us, me aboard the Cat, the others armed with rakes and shovels, set out to clean up dead fish. Lake Michigan—at least our corner of it—was a mess. Alewives by the millions had washed up on the shore, some of the heftier ones bloating on the sand.

Swimmers hated them, and so did the boss. A couple hundred thousand no-good silvery alewives washing up on the beach each day wasn't good for business.

During the height of their spawn, we started the work day on the beach, which bugged us because there were no bikinis out at nine on Lake Michigan. It wasn't a bad job really; we just found the attractions of mid-afternoon more engaging.

I remember that long-ago job because of the psalmist's line "teeming with creatures beyond number." That's what those alewives were. For a month at least, the waves rolled them up continually and turned the beach into a dump full of the shards of a million mirrors. The lunkers were six inches, but most of them were no bigger than your finger. The seagulls ate only their eyes.

The lamprey eel, a hideous-looking thing, was the culprit, hitching itself to game fish and then riding out the host's torturous death. Not pretty. The disappearance of game fish in Lake Michigan in the fifties created a population boom among the alewives.

Today, the lamprey eel is at 10 percent of its peak population because, fifty years ago, researchers discovered a chemical to kill the larvae. Game fish have made a dramatic recovery, and that army surplus Caterpillar has been quietly retired, the lowly alewives devoured by teeming trout and salmon.

Psalm 104 is grand and glowing, a cyclorama almost; but here and there it could use a footnote, I think, and I'm not even an ecologist.

The psalmist is not wrong. There's a great circle in nature, and something links all of us—two-leggeds, four-leggeds, and even those silvery alewife multitudes.

And there is Someone that loves this world so greatly he gave his Son. That's what the Bible suggests in Psalm 104, a long and stunning portrait of the natural world.

But occasionally, I guess, somebody's got to drive an old Cat.

<hr />

When systems go awry in the mechanism of your world, give us the smarts to know how to make it right. You love your creation—that's clear from your Word. You love it—and too often we don't. Forgive us our clumsy trespassing. Fill us with awe. Amen.

WARNING: REWARDS

*"By them your servant is warned; in
keeping them there is great reward."*
—*Psalm 19:11*

When I look back on my life, it seems as if I've been a part of three wholly different eras.

I was a child in the fifties, when, in small-town America, the church was the central institution of our lives, the bona fide authority. Life seemed simple. America had just won a war against genuine evil. Tons of ex-GIs, my father among them, returning from experiences they'd never forget, were looking for little more than sweet peace and quiet security. War's madness gave way to the order of the fifties, everything in its place.

What I remember of Jesus from that time is a visual image almost everyone's seen. A pale glow surrounds his head, a mysterious iridescence from some unseen source. That light is convincing. If you'd ever harbored any doubt about Jesus' divinity, one look at that painting would likely do the trick. You know the drawing—*The Head of Christ*, Warner Sallman, circa 1941.

I grew up in the sixties when authority—church, state, even family—took a beating. Somewhere I have a slide of a kid in a T-shirt, a photo I took on an antiwar march in Washington D.C. On the back of that shirt is a fist with a raised middle finger aimed at just about everything. The guy's my age.

The wall of my office bears a sixties Jesus portrait, this one showing him in a swirl of long hair, his beard bedraggled. He's the sort of guy who would have left on a chopper with Peter Fonda to find America's soul.

I'm growing old in yet another era. This one's not so easy—for me at least—to understand. I have no pictures of Jesus from this era, except for the ones I see in the attitudes of my students. "Jesus, Lover of My Soul" might well be their theme song if they could play it on a keyboard. Jesus in a Starbucks, an exotic dark brew steaming in his hand, a sweet smile over his face, chillin'. Working on relationships.

Which portrait is accurate? Go figure. We're all, at best, fragmentary. Jesus Christ is always bigger, always more complete than whatever fantasy we have going.

Should we, like my students, think of Jesus as a great guy? Should we hook arms with him and break up the military industrial complex, sixties style? And perhaps the most difficult pair of questions of all: Is he someone to love? Is he someone to fear?

There's something striking about the balance in the diction of this verse. I only wish there were a colon where there's a semi-colon now, because I'm thinking that somehow the two sides of the verse go hand in hand. The verse reads like a bizarre highway sign: "Warning: Rewards ahead."

Jaroslav Pelikan, a well-known scholar of the history of Christianity, says that one of the most interesting questions of the Scriptures, one that needs to be answered every decade or so—and maybe more often—was one posed by none other than Jesus Christ: "Who do people say that I am?"

The answer to that question is always the same—and always different, isn't it? As mysteries go, he's the greatest.

But he loves us. Go figure.

＊

There's so much we don't know about you, Lord. But we thank you for what we do know—that you came to this world to live and die in payment for our sin, that you plead our cases now and make a place for us someday. There's so much mystery, but even more grace. Amen.

WANTING

" . . . I shall not want."
—Psalm 23:1, KJV

My friend Diet Eman, who spent more than anyone's fair share of time in a concentration camp in the occupied Netherlands during World War II, won't forget a time every day when the job description of the guards in the prison at Vught changed significantly: instead of beating up on the inmates, the guards had to keep inmates from beating up on themselves.

Because of food. When what little there was emerged, the guards stood by closely. She describes those moments in *Things We Couldn't Say*:

> The only time they watched us closely was when
> we got our bread because resentments could grow
> and tempers flare. If you were assigned the duty of
> cutting margarine, you had to be very careful that all
> the lumps were exactly the same size. . . . You had
> to be very careful slicing it because the others would
> watch very closely. . . . If one slice would have
> been a bit thicker chunk of margarine, there would
> be bickering for sure; when you're hungry, such
> bickering comes easily.

I don't need to document the extremes to which good human beings will go when hungry. Reason gets tossed like cheap wrapping paper in the face of real human need.

I've never been that hungry. Neither have my parents, although, during the Great Depression, they came much closer than I ever did. My mother remembers my grandfather, a squat, big-shouldered blacksmith, crying at supper because neither he nor his farmer customers had any money, and he didn't know where his next dollar was coming from. My father, whose father was a preacher, remembers his parents' cupboards being filled only by the largesse of his congregation.

In my life, "I shall not want" seems a given. Don't even have to ask for what I need—after all, I've got money. In the many years of our marriage, our economic problems have arisen not because of lack of money but because of too much: if our kids need something—even our adult kids—should we buy it for them, or should we make sure they learn some basic lessons in economics? Sometimes—often—our hearts lean one way, our heads the other. Most of the time we don't know what to do.

We have money all right, but of course that doesn't mean we don't need God. We can have the nation's finest filet mignon (we live in beef country, after all) every weekend if we'd like; what's more, Sioux County has the finest pork loin in the world. Food is no problem.

But we *want*—good Lord, do we *want*. We *want* our kids happy. We *want* an end to the dying in Fallujah and Baghdad. We *want* to ease into the pitfalls of old age. We *want* a cottage in Minnesota.

"I shall not want" may be the most audacious claim in all of Scripture because, good Lord, do we ever!

※———※

Lord, I thought I had it down—the difference between wants and needs. But today I'm older, and I know that pulling myself out of the mix is almost impossible. My sin affects it all, Lord. Forgive, forgive, forgive—and help me live anew.
Amen.

THE LEGS OF A MAN

23

*"His pleasure is not in the strength of the horse, nor his
delight in the power of human legs. . . ."*
—*Psalm 147:10*

The athlete in me is well into the fourth quarter. Time's winding down and the game has slowed dramatically. This morning, I'm typing in my athletic shorts, T-shirt, and gym shoes. When my desktop says 5:41, I'll leave for the rec center, where the same folks show up, like me, early Monday, Wednesday, and Friday mornings.

I'll lift weights, get on the steps, then row across a torturous imaginary river before heading home, soaked in sweat, the blessed livery of a workout vet. Tonight, if it's nice, I'll take a walk with my wife—almost three miles. Basically, that's what's left for an aging jock once named "Athlete of the Year" way back in high school. Years ago, I lost the gold cufflinks.

On Friday, I met a sweet kid, a senior in high school who wants to major in English when he gets to college next fall. Turns out his passion is basketball, he says, eyes ablaze. English is OK for a major, but history or math would do the job too, he said. The kid wants to coach.

Could have been me forty years ago.

Great kid. I'd love to have him enroll, whether or not he ever pulls on a jersey. He wants to play ball in college, but he knows making the team is no cakewalk. He says a hotshot from his small Indiana high school came here a few years ago and didn't make the team—so he says he's prepared.

I told him I've seen guys—and women too—hamstrung when suddenly they didn't have to turn up for practice every afternoon of their lives, ex-jocks who said they felt as if bright lights had gone out without the rhythm of after-school practice. I went through that myself—delirium tantrums from no more heavy-laden gym bags. It's identity loss.

He said he knew all of that. He said he thought he was prepared. But, good night, does he want to play!

Psalm 147:10 is a gift for juiced-up jocks, a reminder to a million wannabe all-stars that there's more to life than being MVP or even Charlie Hustle. I tried to tell him as much, but some lessons get learned only by way of personal experience.

This morning when I left the gym, some lanky grade-school kid was shooting free throws. When he went after the ball, his long legs arched a bit like a pair of fine parentheses, the sure sign of speed, athletic gifts. Couldn't help but admire.

But God doesn't care, really. The psalmist says God takes no delight in the power of human legs, whether or not they're as sharply defined as a thoroughbred's.

That's good to hear, especially when mine are all but gone, my knees a foul nest of hooks. We're not loved for the size of our engines or the thrust of our buggy springs. We're loved, even when we've no more horsepower than an old VW bus.

Met a kid last week who told me basketball was his passion. Someday this little verse will bring him comfort, as it does me, an old man who long ago lost his prized cufflinks. It's good to be reminded— at eighteen or fifty-eight—that really, God doesn't much care about all of that.

Bless his holy name.

* * *

The most difficult idols to cast down are not the ones made of stone, Lord, they're the ones we build inside our minds and hearts and souls. Help us to do and be our best. But help us to remember that most of our success means very little to you, the head coach. Thank you for teaching us how to play the game. Amen.

RESTORATION

"He restores my soul."
—Psalm 23:3, NIV

y wife claims she inadvertently got some laughs a week or so ago. At a Bible study on Revelation, she said that, in all honesty, when she thought of heaven she imagined a lakeside cabin in northern Minnesota—preferably not in January.

I know why her friends chuckled.

A friend of mine told me a week ago about his daughter who lives all the way across the state. She and her family have had more than their share of problems—a child with chronic illness, some long-term unemployment, some scrambling for jobs. This daughter, carting her kids to school one day, called her dad from the shoulder of a freeway. The van had thrown in the towel. My friend is a mechanic, but he was also 300 miles away.

I could have never guessed how much time and energy parents expend worrying about adult kids, probably because, even as twenty-somethings, we're all pretty much oblivious to how much worry we can generate—at least I was. Our children also have run into their share of problems—unemployment, physical and emotional strain, scrambling for jobs. And we worry. Do we ever!

Meanwhile, to say the least, we're busy with our own lives—jobs, responsibilities. I'm a church elder; don't ask me if I'm keeping up. I'm on the road too often, and I've always got student papers to read, papers I should have handed back yesterday.

I really should visit my mother more often—she's alone—but she's 500 miles away. My wife's parents aren't as well as they'd like to be. Like many others, my wife and I often feel as sandwiched as salami.

So, for the first time in thirty years, we took a mid-year vacation—slipped silently away to a rented cabin in Minnesota and spent five days in a north woods resplendent in fall colors. The weather was perfect, the leisure was divine.

I was—we were—restored.

For believers, Psalm 23, I'm convinced, is about maintenance. Shepherd that he is, my Lord leads me beside still waters, he makes me lie down, he takes care of me.

Television and politics lie—life is *not* easy. Endless tasks have to be done, and far too often we stub our toes and get paper cuts. We start sagging; parts of us fail. Backs give out. Bladders weaken. It ain't pretty.

But sometimes God gives us these glorious cabin-in-Minnesota moments. He restores us, inside and out. The Lord God almighty blesses us with a cupped hand that holds our lives better than some fancy executive chair. He restores our very soul.

Don't let us run away from restoration, Lord. Don't let us busy ourselves to death, telling each other that our jobs are the only things in life that matter. Bring us to your cottage, Lord. Restore us. Lead us to the lake. Amen.

WAVES AND BREAKERS

". . . All your waves and breakers have swept over me."
—Psalm 42:7

Lots of my students affix Bible verses to their e-mail messages, but the message that sticks with me every time I read it comes from a secretary named Colleen. Her notes always end this way: "You cannot really live until you are ready to die."

I can't know all the reasons why Colleen has attached that particular line to her e-mails, but I think I know one of them: she lost a child. As a parent myself, I can't imagine any single event in any person's life that could be more devastating.

Years ago, when I was a toddler, an aunt of mine was killed in a freakish car accident. I know how hard that death was on my mother, but I never knew how awful it must have been for my grandma until another woman told me a story that happened just a few years later, the story of her own brother's sudden death.

She told me that she'd never forget how my grandma was the first to visit after her brother's death. They were neighbors, so her visit made sense. But I knew why Grandma went to visit her right away. She walked across the street and through her neighbor's back door because she knew exactly what that mother was going through. She could bring real comfort. She'd been there.

I've never known that depth of grief. In some ways, when I look at these words from Psalm 42, I realize I've been blessed with innocence because I've been spared something of the worst.

I remember telling myself, a quarter-century ago, that, should I die on the airplane I was about to board, I could live with that. I knew my wife and little children would go on, that they'd be cared for, that, with time, life would go on without me. That realization on a jetway stair is a moment I've never forgotten. It was an affirmation, in a way. Were I to die, I knew that I could live with who I'd been.

Nothing's changed. Twenty-five years later, I stand by that determination. I honestly believe I can meet Colleen's challenge because I'm ready to die.

What I know now, for the first time in my life, is what a blessing that is, that affirmation. I know it because now I know someone who can't say it because of the ravaging horror of depression. That darkness has taken hold of someone I love as much as Colleen loved her son; and even though I don't know personally the terrors the poet David describes, I do know, and love, someone who does. I've seen the tremors from those breakers. I've felt the waves of darkness storming.

I can only hope and pray that he, like so many others who suffer this darkness, can take heart from this line in an especially memorable psalm—memorable because King David offers us some company in grief.

To know that David knows profound sadness, fear, and despair—and God himself knows, the Father who lost a Son himself—just to know that is a breath of blessed assurance. For Colleen. For Grandma's neighbor. For Grandma herself. For all of us.

We're not alone. That's David's theme here in Psalm 42. And it's the single story of the Bible, I suppose.

Somewhere, right now, many people are suffering through immense losses, losses they never could have dreamed of, waves and breakers that knock them down. Help them stand, Lord God almighty, give them steady breath, a clear eye, courage, and resilience. Give them faith, and bless them with your love. Amen.

FOREVER

"The LORD is enthroned as King forever."
—Psalm 29:10

Yesterday, in an airport, a friend of mine and I were charmed by the members of a high school choir returning from a tour in San Francisco where they'd sung at a number of places, eaten fortune cookies and sourdough bread, and did, they said, all kinds of other fun things. Coming home, those kids were both tired and pumped, as only high school kids can be.

And they were remarkably talkative. We asked some young women if the whole bunch had behaved. They said yes, except for some boys—"but you know how guys are." We asked if there were any tour romances. Only one.

"Maybe that's okay," I quipped. "It's probably good not too many of you left your hearts in San Francisco."

They half-smiled at the old guy. OK, it wasn't a line that would land me a job writing comedy, but I was trying to be catchy. *Trying.* My friend, a guy half my age, looked at me and winced. "I don't think they got that one," he said.

I felt like donating myself to a museum.

Once I reach, say, sixty-nine instead of fifty-nine, I'll be better adjusted to the thud my jokes create. It never dawned on me that those kids might not know a song I thought was imprinted on the American psyche. I simply assumed we shared a world. We don't.

I remember exactly the last time I played basketball. I was pushing thirty. That night, I took a pass from a guard, came across the lane as pumped as those high school kids, and jumped up off my left foot to take a kind of baby hook. But something strange happened. My body, like a sandbag, didn't respond. My mind had me swooping through the air. My body had no notion of the same, and I never stepped on the court again.

Finiteness is something I'm coming to understand far better as I get older. I know it physically, and have for a long time. I know it mentally: words don't come as easily. I know it culturally: my jokes are starting to land as flat as my grandfather's. I know it generationally: my college students say things I simply don't understand, the way my own parents once didn't understand me.

I don't have the power to bend my mind around the word "forever." But I know what David aims to tell us in this verse: God's knees don't buckle. He doesn't forget where he parked his car and hasn't nodded off when he shouldn't have.

God was—and he is—King of creation. Infinite. Forever.

The Lord is enthroned as King *forever*. His kingdom was and is, and forever shall be—world without end. Without fade, without end, without bad jokes.

That's a place to leave your heart.

⊰——⊱

Lord, we are all creatures of time—your gift to us to help us structure our lives. But we take it as our own. Grace us with timelessness. Help us to see eternity. Nothing in our lives— in all of our lives—could be as timely, Lord. Amen.

27

ORDINATION

"If the LORD delights in a man's way,
he makes his steps firm."
—Psalm 37:23 (NIV)

The rough logic of Psalm 37:23 is not that difficult to understand. When—*if*, even—the Lord likes what he sees in us, he'll give us a break. Sounds fair. That's the kind of God I can deal with. He'll love us if he determines we're worth his investment.

But listen to this: "The steps of a man are established by the LORD," says the New American Standard; "and he delights in his way." Or how about the King James: "The steps of a good man are ordained by the LORD, and he delights in his way."

Seems a whole lot different from the New International Version. And the TNIV changes it even more. Correct me if I'm wrong, but in the gap that separates the translations, you could float a whale. In the NIV, something reciprocal is occurring—"you scratch my back, I'll scratch yours." That kind of thing sounds as if God almighty is shopping for a used car—kicking tires, checking mileage, looking for dings. If he likes what he sees, he makes an offer.

In the King James, God isn't shopping. He's turning out human beings, setting them on a charted course, and watching them move where he's determined they would, like spinning tops. But even that's a lousy analogy because, once spun, the top-spinner has no idea of direction. Maybe he's like one of those guys who loves model trains. Get the cars out of the box, assemble the tracks, and set 'em on a path that won't change unless you reassemble the set.

In the KJV and New American Standard, God seems to know where we go, when we stand, and when we stoop—our ups and downs and all arounds. What's more, he delights in watching *us* ambulate. He loves to watch us circle around the tracks he's laid.

That's a whole different God from the one who's looking for used cars — or so it seems.

At bottom is a pair of contrary ideas that have puzzled human beings for centuries. Are we free, or is everything about us preconceived, foreordained, predestined? Good folks, brilliant theologians, learned scholars have and will continue to disagree, I'm sure — as do the Bible translators.

What did the poet king say? Where would he come down? What did he intend? Whose translation is accurate?

Those questions don't bother me greatly because this is, first of all, a song, not a conference presentation. Psalm 37 is about security, about comfort, about feeling rest and peace in the Popeye arms of the One who made us and who never leaves us.

In the very next verse David will admit he's an old guy, a fact which may be key to our accepting the sheer joy of this line's upholstered comfort. I'm probably about as old as he was when he wrote the song or offered the meditation. And I think I know why he wouldn't care for the whole debate. Really, all David wants us to know is that when he looks back on his life — all of it — he knows for sure that God will never leave him alone.

Verse 23, no matter how you read it, is far less a proposition than it is a promise — that God was there always, and will be forever.

———※———

I don't know a whole lot, Lord, and the older I get I'm less sure of what I once thought I knew. But this much is clear: If I look behind me, I see you — and when I look ahead, there you are too. I'm not always sure of the right now, Lord, but it's great comfort to know that in every other direction you're the only real presence in my life. Amen.

THE KEEPER

"The LORD will keep you from all harm —
he will watch over your life."
Psalm 121:7

My father was an elder in the church, but I knew very little about what happened when he walked off to meetings. Most of what went on he was sworn not to tell. Some of it he didn't tell me because the knowledge would have hurt me. I was, after all, a child.

One part of his job was tallying after communion. He'd meet with the other elders after the Lord's Supper to determine who was there, who wasn't, and who was purposefully not taking the elements. I have no idea what the elders called that little gumshoe reconnaissance, but I know that they met. It was a whole different era. Those elders were watching for people who were coming to the table with a checkered past—or who were creating a checkered present.

When I became an elder, nobody watched the sacrament that closely. Maybe I remember what went on back then because I knew that there were stories I would have liked to know. I'd still like to know. Whatever the reason, I remember that he'd come back home late after communion Sunday worship.

That post-communion tallying—as well as my father's own righteousness—may be responsible for my deeply rooted sense that elders should be godly men or women, dutiful, virtuous, and devout. And that conviction may be why, more than any other elderly task, I have always loved distributing the elements, giving away the body and blood of Jesus Christ. It's a big job meant for the kind of person who grows into the office, having raised good kids, having been the spouse of only one mate, with no messes in the scrapbook.

But last night I received the sacrament from two men who were once thugs, criminals. Two men who, for many years, valued only their own skin. Last night I took the bread and wine from people who cheated others, stole what they could to line their pockets, used drugs, and lived promiscuously. At about the time I began to understand why my father came home late after communion services, they were leaving behind a childhood they never had in a Southeast Asian war zone.

I know them. I've walked into their lives year by year, even written their stories. I know that those men—the ones who offered bread and wine last night—were once so far gone in treachery that not a soul in our church could have imagined some of the villainy they'd perpetuated. Who'd have thought they'd someday be doling out the body and blood of Christ? Amazing.

But the promise of Scripture, and the Word of the Lord here in Psalm 121, is that the Lord will keep us from harm—he will watch over our life. All during those bloody years in war-torn Laos, where those two men grew up, God almighty had his eye on them as if they were fledgling sparrows, even when—especially when—they were lousy thugs.

He knew them. He was watching them, keeping them from harm, even when they were yet sinners.

Last night, those two guys fed me the body and blood of Jesus. Amazing grace. What a celebration! What a savior!

Just about everyone loves "Amazing Grace," Lord—you don't even have to be a believer. But only believers know how you've taken us in when we were sinners, how you made a place for us in your family, how you show us the way home. Thanks, forever. Amen.

REMEMBRANCES

". . . you thought I was exactly like you."
—Psalm 50:21

Years ago, when I was in high school, my uncle—a most distinguished uncle—came to visit. He took me golfing. I'd fooled around with golf clubs since I was ten, I'm sure, but my family was never part of the country club set back then, and actually going to a course would have been, well, out of the question. A frivolous use of our money, my father would have said.

After nine holes, my uncle wanted to ride out in the countryside around the town of Oostburg, Wisconsin, where I was growing up, and he had too, maybe thirty-five years before. His career had led him afar from his geographic roots, and I could tell that it was a joy for him to reminiscence while touring the old haunts.

"Now go west of town," he told me, and I did, then followed the river. "There," he said. "See that path through the field? If you follow that road, you'll come to a swimming hole." He was overflowing with memory. "Ever been there? Great place—we used to have so much fun." And then he was gone, lost in memory.

I was the very age he was remembering himself being. I remember thinking it odd that he could be so emotionally attached to a bend in the river I'd never seen, even though we'd both grown up in the same neighborhood. There'd been spectacular fun there years before, but no one I knew ever frequented that place. He knew the world in which I was growing up, but it was almost a different country.

Yesterday a friend of mine who also grew up in Oostburg, Wisconsin, came back to his home on the edge of the plains. Even before he left, he was down because his parents had decided to move across the lake to Michigan, and he was afraid that this Oostburg visit might well be his last.

It's a rite of passage I know. When my parents left the house in which I grew up, some kind of emptiness descended, even though they were simply moving across town. But my uncle's visit years ago, when I witnessed his reverence for a spot on the river I'd never visited, had prepared me for that leave-taking.

The gulf that divides reality and perception can be immense. The town my uncle knew wasn't the place where I grew up, nor is it the place my friend doesn't want to forget. We're all diaspora finally; none of those Oostburgs exist today.

The worlds we imagine aren't the ones we live in. Similarly, I suppose, the God we imagine isn't necessarily the one who exists through time and eternity. In a psalm that's frequently shocking, here's yet another line to make us sweat: "You thought I was exactly like you."

God's not what we think—that's what he's reminding us. Not much is, of course; but you can bet that's true of God. He's altogether divine, and from what we read in the Old Testament, he is certainly no teddy bear. The fact is, we really don't know him.

Perhaps I find that disconcerting because I've created an image of him in my own mind as a genial gentleman who's really into forgiveness.

"You thought I was exactly like you," that God says. I think I have. I just hope I'm right.

⋙⋙✕⋘⋘

Some of the finest lessons of life, Lord, come when we find out we were wrong. We think we're right about you, but we know that you are God and we aren't. We also know—by your Word—that you love us. And that's all we really need to know. Amen.

MERCY

"Have mercy on me, my God, have mercy on me,
for in you I take refuge."
—Psalm 57:1

Psalm 57 is not about sin. Forgiveness is not at stake here. David may well have reason to cower in the face of the almighty, but that's not what's going on. He's tired and oppressed; he's sick of the deadly cops-'n-robbers game he's got going with King Saul, the Lord's anointed. David can't see his way out of it. He's tried to be charitable; when he could have killed the king he only cut out a chunk of the king's robe instead.

But nothing's changed. He's still on the run, along with dozens of his people, as he has been for too long. They're all refugees, scared to death. He's got nowhere to turn in a cold, wet cave, so he goes to his God. "Have mercy on me," he says, "for in you I take refuge."

A man stood up in our church last week to ask for our prayers. It was very painful to listen to him stammer, one of those moments when you wonder whether we should so easily spill out our guts in such a public forum. He and his wife have a baby on the way, and a doctor· had told them that week that the baby wasn't healthy. I'm not sure exactly what the problem is, but it was clear that the world that family had been living in had been shaken deeply by the news of their baby's precarious health.

Later, I was told that the mother—the father had done all the talking—was telling people she simply wasn't sure anymore that God existed. It probably never dawned on them that there were other families with kids with significant problems sitting right there listening, not to mention the kids themselves.

I don't worry about that woman or that family. I know mothers in our church (fathers too, of course), people who've got kids with problems, who would gladly take her hand, hug her, and let her know that sometimes great blessings are not all that beautifully wrapped.

Which is not to say that anyone would tell her that her life, from this point on, is going to be a piece of cake. Some people are specially blessed to be able to say to people like that scared young mother that what lies in wait for them around blind corners isn't what they might fear or despise or even recognize. They know. They too have suffered.

Maybe — I don't know — this young family with their two beautiful children has never before sat outside a cave like David did, the morning sun or an evening sky laid out before him promising a silence that he just can't know, besieged by seemingly insurmountable problems. Maybe it's the first time this young couple has felt really beat up.

Maybe I don't worry all that much about them because of David, sitting in that cave with a chunk of robe in his hand. He's convinced he did the right thing in sparing the king's life — knowing, as he does, that his own life is imperiled because of the king's envy and pride. There seems no way out. "Mercy," he cries.

At one point or another in our lives, all of us will cry for mercy at the open and dark mouth of a cave, I believe. And God hears our cry.

You know that we need your love and strength every day of our lives. You know that without faith, some of us would simply disintegrate. You know we need your grace. But there are some days when the level of need grows way, way out of control. Be with us especially then, on those days — and months, and, for some of us, years. Like nothing else, in those times, we covet your abiding love. We ask these things in the name of your Son. Amen.

HALF-FULL

*"As they pass through the Valley of Baka, they make it
a place of springs; the autumn rains also cover it with
pools. They go from strength to strength,
till each appears before God in Zion."*
—*Psalm 84:6-7*

This afternoon, I'll fly off to British Columbia. In the
next few days I'm scheduled to do a number of things,
including visiting some folks in an independent living
facility called Elim Home—a couple dozen or more
seniors who want to hear me read a story. That's the
plan.

Word got out. The good folks at Elim Home got the news that a
writer was coming to read something he'd written, a man who'd often
written things in their church magazine. "You know him, maybe, eh?
He's from a long ways away—from Iowa, in the States—and he's
coming to Elim Home. Ja, sure."

Lots of immigrant brogues in this place.

One of them phoned the man who arranged my schedule on this
visit.

"Ve vere vondering," he told him, "whether Mr. Schaap might come
a little early and help us learn to write our own stories."

Some requests simply aren't to be denied.

I'm not sure why, but that polite request makes me smile. Maybe
it's because I just finished another couple of semesters of teaching.
Sometimes—not all the time; I don't want to overstate—coming into
class can be like walking into a wake. Not a single student in the room
is really interested in Ralph Waldo Emerson. But this Vancouver class,
this gaggle of seniors, they want *more* time, not less, *more* attention,
not less. They want to learn. I know, I know—I sound really whiny.

But the possibility of assuaging my wounded pride is not the only reason the request from Elim Home has made my week. The other is simply what it is those folks are demanding: they want help writing their stories. Good night, they're all seniors, and they're just now getting started thinking seriously about writing their life stories. There's something so good, so strong, so hearty about a home full of old folks wanting to learn. That they want to is unmitigated blessing.

It seems the older I get, the more I have to learn to pay attention to those kinds of blessings or I miss them altogether. Honestly, the prospect of visiting a couple dozen retired Dutch immigrants who want to write their life stories—it's sheer joy to consider. It's a peppermint in a snoozy sermon. It's enough to make me smile.

I don't know that anyone has a clue about the Valley of Baka, although I'd guess some Bible scholars would be happy to hazard a theory. But then, I'm not sure that the relative glories of that place are all that important to understanding the psalm. At the heart of these verses of Psalm 84 is a tribute to people who pay attention to joy, who let it fill them, who let it carry them over the dark places.

These are people of pilgrimage, who take their strength from God, whose very footsteps make the desert bloom. These are people who sing in the rain. And tomorrow I'll be blest by being among 'em.

Lord, thanks for the good days, the good things, the sweet things, the take-your-breath-away moments. Help me to see them more often because I know they're there. Most of the time, I'm just not taking the time to look. Thanks for joy.
Amen.

THE ONES THAT RUN OUR LIVES

"... may [my willful sins] not rule over me...."
—Psalm 19:13

I was old enough to know better, but *knowing* assumes some modicum of reason, and reason, that night, was not in the building.

There was a peephole between our rooms. I don't know who found it. There were five of us in one room, and four or five of them next door. We were men—well, boys. They were female. We didn't know them. As fate would have it, we had rented adjoining rooms in an old frame boarding house on the lakefront, the kind of place Al Capone may have frequented running from the law.

The hole was up high enough in the closet to require a chair. I can't imagine how anyone found it, but one of us did. They were sitting on the beds in that room in various states of undress, and the view from that little peephole couldn't have been sweeter if we'd had one of those bulky mechanical binoculars on the frothy banks of the Niagara. Some of those images are still in the scrapbook in my head.

But not one of us could stay up on the chair long enough to get any real footage because the others would drag him down. King of the Mountain is what it became, except the closet wars were fought in furtive silence—no one wanted the girls to know they were being watched—*ogled* is the word, I guess.

Then something strange happened. The struggle got way out of hand. Good buddies became enemies; the sights beyond that closet wall were too great a delight to let anyone hog the chair. Testosterone-laden, we ripped each other down and climbed over each other fiercely for one more glorious peek.

This is nuts—this is really nuts, I thought, even as I scraped my way back up to the top. I couldn't help myself. Since that time I've always felt a little cautious critiquing Sigmund Freud because at that moment there was little to separate us from the beasts of the field, and maybe I'm dissing rabbits when I say it.

Was it sin to look at undressed girls? I certainly knew better. But the fierce emotions, I remember, were scary, even at the moment I was their victim.

Think of King David, spotting Bathsheba in the tub on some adjoining rooftop, and later sending Uriah to his death. Reason be hanged—we got to have what we got to have.

An alcoholic friend of mine told me that only once he got sober did he realize that he'd planned his entire day around drinking—one during lunch, another at coffee, another before home, then again at night, a snort on the bottle he kept furtively in the washroom, and so on. Presumptuous sin can be controlling, and only its victims will deny it.

"He who sups with the devil," the old saying goes, "had best use a long spoon." Our presumptuous sins can rule over us far worse than bad habits.

David has already asked the Lord to forgive him for those sins he doesn't know about himself—and they're there. Now he's talking about those other sins, the ones we know but do anyway, the ones that run our lives, the ones that we do, reason be hanged, conscience be snuffed. Those sins, Lord, he pleads—don't let them rule our hearts.

David knows himself, and he knows us. And, thank goodness, he knows the Lord!

The great sins of the spirit—pride, envy, wrath—are sometimes the most difficult to perceive because they come to us so humanly. But there are others, Lord, the ones we know better than to commit. But we do them anyway, drawn by another spirit altogether. In the heat of our human passions, Lord, keep us cool. Keep us in your love. And, always, as you've promised, forgive us our sins. Amen.

WHOSE SIN IS COVERED

"Blessed are those . . . whose sins are covered."
—Psalm 32:1

After far too much traveling in the last couple of years, I have come to the conclusion that motel rooms are not designed for people my age; they are decorated with entirely too many mirrors. Wherever you look, full-length panels of reflective glass offer you entirely unbidden views of your own sagging mortality.

One of the reasons English comedies are so much funnier than American sitcoms is that English audiences, it seems, don't demand physical perfection. English comedies regularly feature unhandsome people; but American television offers a persistent diet of perfect shapes, both male and female—so many, in fact, that one begins to believe such pulchritude is the norm. Given all that gorgeous flesh, suddenly seeing yourself bare-naked on a six-foot wall is an epiphany of horrific proportions.

A few weeks ago I came home and told my wife I would never eat again.

I suppose I shouldn't be equating sin with the body. But there's a link here, at least in my mind. The exuberance of this verse from Psalm 32 bursts from the realization that something hideous, revolting, and humiliatingly repulsive is taken care of, covered up, covered over, put out of sight—even better, out of mind and soul. That something isn't nakedness, but it's close.

Sin, of course, isn't so much an act as it is a condition, like dandruff. It's something we never stop fighting. There's no truth, says the apostle Paul, in those who claim they have no sin.

The blissful joy of the opening lines of Psalm 32—or so it seems to me—is not the blessed realization that our sinful *condition* is gone but instead our blessed assurance that God's forgiveness has covered up, like whiteout, something really evil that we *did*. That sin—the one we can't forget, the one that haunts us day and night, the one that makes us sick unto death—*that* sin, in all its pathetic naked horror, is what's covered. It's not visible. It's buried. It's gone. By the miracle of grace, it honestly never happened.

David's sin, the unsavory mess created when he couldn't keep his royal hands off someone else's wife, and how—so humanly—he sought to "cover" that sin by the sleazy second-hand murder of her beloved, is legendary.

All of that is gone, he says. It's absolutely and eternally history.

The triumphant joy of the first line of this psalm is the fundamental melody of the good news. Our sin—what we did when we thought no one was looking, or what we did brazenly when the whole world's eyes were open—*that* sin is covered, it's ground into nothingness, it's vanished. Our greed, our neglect, our thievery, our hate, our drunkenness, our adultery, our pathetic pride, our green-eyed jealousy—all those are covered. Our revolting nakedness will never be seen again, no matter how tall the mirrors.

What's left in its place is beauty, the beauty of grace. Praise the Lord.

If the image in the mirror corresponds in any way to the image of our souls, Lord, we're in big trouble. Thank you for forgiveness, for making us new, for giving us eternal beauty. Amen.

BE EXALTED

"Be exalted, O God, above the heavens;
let your glory be over all the earth."
—Psalm 57:11

ook my breath away. Honestly, it did. A quarter-century ago, I was on the very edge of what Canadians call "the bush," in a 1930s farm home in northern Ontario with twenty-some people. Fifteen or so were members of one family, all of them smiling. I was a guest, the youth retreat speaker, along with a half-dozen others, kids on retreat. When the dad prayed that first morning at breakfast, I felt the blessing.

One afternoon Dad and his boys butchered a cow. I walked out back to watch. When one of the boys got on the tractor and scooped up the entrails, I asked another where he was toting that blood and guts. "We'll dump it out back," he said. I shook my head in the loud sputtering of the tractor. "The bears'll get it," he yelled over the popping engine.

A wilderness family of seventeen people so full of love and spirit I wished the world could take a seat at that long kitchen table and get their own breakfast scoop of porridge. Faith breathed in that house and beamed out there in the bush; and I knew, maybe for the first time in my life, that I had to commit what I felt to words.

A few days ago, twenty-five years and a half-dozen visits later, I returned from the mom's funeral. Her husband had died just a few months before.

It's a long ride up to the bush, and we got there just before ten at night. The wake was just about over. They'd kept the coffin open for us, they said, because they knew we were coming. And there she was, mom to fifteen kids and fifty-plus grandchildren, most of them there in the church. Her mortal shell was there, but she was gone, somewhere smiling.

Her sons had built the gorgeous coffin, and once we backed away, the six of them together closed the lid. I've seen wreaths laid at Arlington's Tomb of the Unknown Soldier, but those six strong men bringing the cover down over their mom's remains, a cover they'd made with their own hands, was a loving gesture I'll never forget.

Honestly, I'm not sure what David means when he asks the Lord to exalt himself. It's as if he's trying to coax some jittery kid out on the stage for a show that's been rehearsed for weeks. I'm still not sure God almighty needs a cheerleader. "Be exalted, Lord," he says, as if the Creator of heaven and earth is somehow introverted.

But this morning I'm thinking that the glory of the Lord is not just a perfect dawn or some stupendous miracle that leaves us speechless. The God I know is exalted in the lives of his saints, each of them, and in their going home, all that devoted joy left behind.

Three days ago I attended the funeral of a deeply pious woman, the mother of fifteen, who, long ago, with her husband, made me want to sing in a house on the edge of the bush with bears for neighbors. Three days ago, up there in the wilderness again, I saw, for the last time, a woman on whom God's glory shone like a sparkling patina.

I don't think David had a funeral in mind when he ended this wholehearted psalm of praise with the words he did, but I believe he'd be singing himself at the blessed eternity of the lives of the saints, one more of whom is now home.

In her annual joy at first robins and early daffodils, in her unceasing prayers for her children, in her lifelong trust in the Lord, that woman, a cheerleader in God's glorious wilderness, praised the Lord. God almighty was and is exalted.

***

Thank you for people who exalt your name by the ordinary righteousness of their own ordinary lives. Thank you for witnesses, a cloud of them, living and dead, who can testify to their joy in being a member of your blessed family. Bless us with strength to be among them. Amen.

WHEN?

"What right have you to recite my laws or take my covenant on your lips? You hate my instruction and cast my words behind you."
—Psalm 50:16-17

Not that many years ago, a student who liked to haunt my office was talking about her church, one of the new ones, full of raised hands and happy faces. "You'd like it," she told me. "You really would—you ought to try it sometime."

Like a new flavor of cappuccino.

She shrugged her shoulders. "But every once in a while—when I get all up or something—then I need to go back to Bethel," she said, referring to a church with a more traditional worship style, "just to settle my nerves, you know?"

That was my introduction to a phenomenon described on the front page of this morning's *New York Times* online edition: "Church to Church—Teenagers Seek Church That Fits." The article goes on to explain this kind of church-shopping—church-hopping, really—being done, reportedly, by hundreds of thousands of evangelical Christian teenagers, including my own students.

Their parents approve, the *Times* reported. Believing parents long for nothing on this earth more than their kids' growing relationship with Jesus Christ. One mother, whose Netherlandic name suggests she was born in the same Calvinist order I was, is quoted as follows: "I saw that my parents' relationship to Christ and my relationship to Jesus Christ were different, and my kids aren't going to relate to Jesus Christ the same way we do," said Emily's mother, Tracy Hoogenboom, 49. "And that's to be expected because Jesus Christ is your own personal Lord and Savior."

Makes sense. But sometimes I wonder how believers like Tracy Hoogenboom read passages like Psalm 50. Forget the vituperation and the lines in the sand God almighty draws so succinctly? Forget the false recitation and the bogus covenant-making? Forget vanity and snake oil?

I wonder, simply, what some believers do with the tone of voice God uses in Psalm 50. Does that mother think about the snarling God of Psalm 50 as her daughter's "personal Lord and Savior"? Or is that just Jesus?

"All that's left is ego," a friend of mine, a preacher, told me recently. In the withering of established institutions (church, school, family, and bowling team) created by our myopic affluence, all that's left is ego, is self—almighty "choice." It's the only real commodity. We've got to get our needs met.

When Christ describes separating people to his left and to his right, he explains that his actions are based on their behavior toward the needy. Neither sheep nor goats have a clue why they're being sent to heaven or hell. "When did we see you hungry or lame or in prison?" both groups say, bewildered.

What strikes terror in my soul when I read Psalm 50's vision of an irate God is that it seems impossible for me to see myself as the recipient of God's rage. After all, when did I falsely recite God's laws? When did I not treasure his covenant? When did I not take him seriously, for pity's sake? When did I slough off his words?

I don't remember any such thing.

<hr />

Forgive my sins, Lord, especially the ones I'm blind to. Like pride. Like thinking I'm really quite a good guy. For I know that all have sinned, that none are innocent, that we all need grace—maybe most when we'd like to believe we don't. Forgive us our sins, Lord. We're asking in Jesus' name.
Amen.

THOSE WHO TAKE REFUGE

"The LORD helps them and delivers them;
he delivers them from the wicked and saves them,
because they take refuge in him."
—Psalm 37:40

S he was one of four African Americans on a city bus in Montgomery, Alabama, that day in December 1955. One of four African Americans seated in a section of the bus that was something of a twilight zone, a place blacks could sit as long as there weren't too many white passengers.

The front of the bus was reserved for white people; the back was for blacks. In much of the American South, Jim Crow was still the law of the land.

She'd been working all day at the department store, and she was tired—physically tired but also spiritually tired, her soul bruised by the treatment of her people. Treatment she'd experienced ever since she was old enough to understand the parameters of the racial divide in the world in which she lived.

She and her husband were members of the local NAACP, active in civil rights cases. What she did that day when she refused to give up her seat to a white man simply because he was white may well have been spur-of-the-moment, but it wasn't without context. "I don't think I should have to stand up," she told the bus driver, who was trying to get her to move. She stayed put because, she said to an interviewer a few months later, "I would have to know for once and for all what rights I had as a human being and a citizen of Montgomery, Alabama." She knew what was at stake.

Her name was Rosa Parks, and today as I write she'll be buried in Detroit, the city she called home since 1957. She goes to her grave as the woman many call "the mother of racial integration" in America.

Rosa Parks has rightly become as much a part of the American story as George Washington's cherry-tree honesty or Ben Franklin's penniless arrival in Philadelphia.

Three other African Americans gave up their seats, in all likelihood, for good reason—they stayed out of jail. A dozen white people didn't think twice when she was removed from that bus. Maybe some of them never even glanced up from their papers. None of them had any idea that race relations in their city and their nation were going to change, powered by a one woman's refusal to leave her bus seat.

Few stories are as important in twentieth-century American history.

Today, at her funeral, Aretha Franklin will sing "How Great Thou Art," Rosa Parks's favorite hymn. It's probably fair to say that most of America would be willing to sing those four words in tribute to Rosa Parks—"Rosa, how great *thou* art."

But Rosa Parks gave God all the raves. "I believe in church and my faith," she wrote in *Quiet Strength*, "and that has helped to give me the strength and courage to live as I did."

Last week Rosa Parks died. Today she'll be buried. But her life inspires millions. She's an authentic American hero and a testimony to the truth of the words King David uses, as yet another promise, to end this long psalm.

It's about the comfort coming to those who seek shelter—as Rosa Parks did, in the bounty of God's love.

Lord, thank you for the inspiration of truly courageous people. Forgive us for our blindness, for the times we don't see obvious injustice. Thank you for witnesses. Thank you for Rosa Parks, for her faith, her drive, her commitment to righteousness and the poor. Bless us with others. Bless our kids with others still to walk on the streets where we live. Give them giant heroes of the faith. In Jesus' name we pray. Amen.

THE HEATHEN

"Many are the woes of the wicked. . . ."
—*Psalm 32:10*

Maybe so. Maybe not.

Proportionally, do the wicked suffer more or less than the righteous? I'm not sure. Some forms of suffering the righteous undergo aren't even background music in the lives of really bad people. After all, only the righteous know when they've messed up.

But that's a topic for another time. Right now, give me a minute to brag about my granddaughter.

My son and his longtime girlfriend came to a relatively congenial parting of the ways recently. It was tough on him. My guess is that it was tough on her too, but I know it was tough on my granddaughter, who'd come to nearly worship the ground this young lady walked upon.

How does one explain a break-up to a four-year-old? Her father told her that, well, people change. That seemed to help.

The next day at day care, she ambled up to her teacher with the news that her uncle wasn't with his girlfriend anymore.

"Oh, really," the teacher said.

"Well, you know," Jocelyn said, deadly serious, "people change."

Her teacher told Jocey's mom that she had all she could do not to laugh.

I don't know whether Jocelyn was telling her teacher a truth she'd totally digested, or if her mind was acting like a tape recorder. But if she did understand her father's explanation, I'm pleased, because at four years old she's arrived at the level of wisdom that many don't achieve until much later, if at all.

We're talking about *wisdom* here. That's a word brought to mind by today's passage, because I'm not as sure as David that the claim he offers is exactly right. In my world, the wicked aren't always woeful; sometimes, like it or not, they prosper.

We don't have to look all that far to find an entirely contradictory appraisal right here in the Psalms. "They have no struggles; their bodies are healthy and strong," says Psalm 73. "They are free from the burdens common to man; they are not plagued by human ills." No woes there.

The Bible is less squeamish about contradiction than we are. What seems true in one verse seems a whole lot less so just down the block. How do we make sense of such things?

In his "Introduction to the Wisdom Books" in *The Message*, Eugene Peterson claims that "the Psalms are indiscriminate in their subject matter—complaint and thanks, doubt and anger, outcries of pain and outbursts of joy, quiet reflection and boisterous worship." It's all here in this book. "If it's human," he says, "it qualifies."

The richness of David's somewhat immodest claim in this line is not that it is forever true. The essential joy that follows his claim about the woes of the wicked is the happiness he feels in forgiveness. About the specifics, maybe he's not to be trusted; after all, he sings a different song later in the concert.

But about the big picture in Psalm 32—the triumph of forgiveness—he's on the money. About that, he has every good reason to brag.

Relieve us from covetousness when the merry unfaithful get all the headlines, Lord. Keep us from envy when the rich get richer. Fill us with grace so that we see things for what they are, truth for what it is, life for what it truly offers. Keep us humble and satisfied, content and comforted. Keep us from sin. This we ask in the name of one who never coveted, our Lord Jesus. Amen.

WHEN THE WICKED PROSPER

". . . Do not fret when people succeed in their ways,
when they carry out their wicked schemes."
—Psalm 37:7

Just a few years ago, the college where I teach celebrated its fiftieth birthday. I was up to my ears, traveling the length and breadth of this continent drumming up whatever enthusiasm I could. It was great fun, but I'm glad it's over.

There would be no college here if its first president had never taken a call to serve a local church. His name was Bernard J. Haan, and he was a stem-winder. He made national news in the late forties by keeping a movie house out of town. To him and his denomination, movies—like cards and dancing—were what people used to call "worldly," as in, "of this world."

I have a picture of him holding forth in front of the church where I worship, a young man full of hellfire. That he loved the camera is obvious from the fact that he took up such a brimstone pose for a *Time* magazine reporter.

I need to come clean about my heritage. There's a mean streak in me about movies that likely harks back several generations to clergymen grandfathers of mine—two of them—who were probably convinced that Hollywood was Babylon.

Their opinions lost currency eventually. I've watched movies my whole life; my son is doing graduate studies—in film. That doesn't mean I don't have a touch of my grandfathers' DNA, though, because sometimes I think the entire world would be better off if that California kahuna earthquake, when it finally comes, tumbles Hollywood deep into the Pacific.

A couple summers ago, the box office biggie was a remake of an idiotic TV show from the eighties — *The Dukes of Hazzard*. It was stupid when it was on TV. If you listen to critics, Hollywood updated even more dopiness into the story — nothing but car chase silliness and constant cleavage.

It made millions. A review in our local paper gave it half of a star out of a possible five. But it also took most of a page to say that. It's the buzz that counts, of course. That movie got more ink in last week's paper than famine in the Sudan. It's no wonder bin Laden and his hosts hate us. This is the freedom that's our gift to the world?

Don't get me started.

I wonder if B. J. Haan was all that wrong about Hollywood — that's what I'm saying. In American culture today, among the most wicked (I know I'm being judgmental) are those who spew Hollywood offal. I know, I know — I sound like an old fogy.

This verse from Psalm 37, however, isn't about my righteousness or Hollywood's corruption. It says, "do not fret," so forgive me my invective. I'm not listening closely. When *Dukes of Hazzard* makes millions, we shouldn't get in a huff — that's what David says. When the wicked prosper, we shouldn't cry. It's all a flash in the pan.

Besides, that summer's most incredible sleeper was an elegant love story about devotion among emperor penguins, not a car chase in two whole hours.

Fifty years after B. J. held forth, there's a theater in my town, and it's busy most of the time. I'm not sure we're better off, but I've been there myself, and I don't fret.

Much.

⋙✕⋘

Relieve us from our unnecessary angst, Lord. We know you're in charge. We know this is your world and we are your people. We know what is good and right and true. Keep us strong and resistant to the siren songs in our culture, and keep our kids above the fray. Bless us all. Amen.

SATISFACTION

*"Satisfy us in the morning with your unfailing love,
that we may sing for joy and be glad all our days."*
—Psalm 90:14

Received an e-mail late last night from friends, a retired pastor and his wife. They told me the news of their son who's fifty-three, their oldest child. A few weeks ago he started feeling a bit weak, they say, and went in for tests that turned up something significant. The specialist who saw him identified the problem as ALS, also known as Lou Gehrig's disease.

There is some hope, as some who suffer ALS can keep on going for a long time. Others, of course, don't. "Won't get into numbers," they wrote—or rather the mother did. Right now, their son "has to be pulled up out of his big comfortable chair if he wants to get up. Has to use a walker. Totally weak arms and legs so far. Can hardly pick up his arm or hold spoons when he eats. We go see him . . . often."

Friends from work and church come visit him at home, she says, and he keeps a positive outlook. "He will enjoy each day as they go along." Their son has three little grandchildren who live almost next door. "They perk him up," the note says. His wife is wonderful and caring. She pushes the wheelchair when they go anywhere. And then this: "So . . . it is finally sinking in to me that this is happening to our oldest 'child.' I seem to call him 'Danny Boy' now."

All of that, just last night, late.

That Moses would write this line makes sense: "Satisfy us in the morning with your unfailing love, that we may sing for joy and be glad all our days."

It's almost impossible to read the story of the Exodus and not be a little anti-Semitic. After all God had done for them, taking down

Pharaoh and his minions in the Red Sea, then establishing his own tent right there among them, thereby granting them the glory of his presence, those Israelites still found things to moan about.

Yahweh splashes manna around every morning, and they want duck in wine sauce. He gives them duck and they want sirloin. Is it any wonder God got sick of them, told them an entire generation had to die before he'd bring them home? The Israelites give Jews a bad name.

Once, at a burning bush, God instructed Moses to speak for him — *and*, in a way, to speak for his people before Pharaoh. In Psalm 90, that's what Moses is doing. He's speaking for them and himself, and certainly for all of us. He's asking for something few of us ever get — real satisfaction.

And I have an e-mail to prove it. I don't know Danny Boy, his kids, his darling grandkids, or his loving, caring wife. But I know his parents, and I know at least something of their sadness. I wish they weren't suffering. I wish Danny Boy wasn't dying. I wish those grandkids weren't losing a grandfather. Some things just aren't right in the world.

Moses' prayer resonates because we all know the impulse: "Satisfy us," he begs. It's the song we all sing, every day of our lives.

Except, maybe, Danny Boy, who will, as he says, "enjoy each day as they go along."

⬥

As the psalm says, Lord, "teach us to number our days."
Give us the heart for wisdom and keep us satisfied, even
when what goes on all around makes us feel emptied.
"Satisfy us in the morning with your unfailing love." Amen.

MY GLORY

"How long will you men turn my glory into shame?"
—*Psalm 4:2*

A ll prayer, our preacher said yesterday, is praise. Even our anguish, our laments, our anger at God— it's all praise because we wouldn't be praying if we didn't actually believe that God is God. All prayer is praise— every phrase, every groan. We're acknowledging God, we're asking him, we're talking to him because we know he's there.

That helps me understand what's going on in Psalm 4:2: "How long will you men turn my glory into shame?"

I've got an assortment of old trophies sitting around my desk here—a couple of little gold basketball players, three golf trophies, and one gold baseball player who's been sitting here, bat cocked, waiting for a pitch that hasn't come for thirty-five years.

On the wall to my right is my diploma. The wall behind me holds several framed book covers—my books. It sounds awful, but I've decorated my study with my glory.

But when David bemoans the fact that those men are turning his glory into shame, he's not ticked off because someone's given his poetry a bad review or editorialized against his kingship. I don't think he means anything personal by "my glory."

Elsewhere in the psalms, many have argued, phrases like this point at the Lord. David's "glory" is really in his salvation, in knowing that the Lord listens to his prayers. His glory is not in his trophies; his glory, quite simply, *is* the Lord.

So for all this psalm's emotional meandering, it's about concern, about the sadness that rises in all of us when we know that people we really admire don't serve the Master. Psalm 4 is not about David but about love, God's love, which is David's glory.

Honestly, the whole of Psalm 4 seems like an emotional roller-coaster to me—not well suited for a man my age. It moves all over the map.

However, David's song may well be not as reckless as it first seems if we understand that this accusation in verse 2 does not rise from a pity party (and he did have some of those), but instead from his deep regard for the rotten directions seemingly good people, people he admires, are taking.

In some ways, I think, this psalm is about enlisting the help of the Lord in the heartfelt attempt to bring your friends home.

I am thrilled to know that an old novelist friend of mine prayed in the last few moments of his life. I loved the guy. He was a literary father to me, a great joy; but I honestly didn't know about his faith. Today, however, I know this much from an unimpeachable source: on his deathbed, he and his nurse prayed together. My joy is God's glory in bringing him a nurse who prayed with him—and who would tell me.

All prayer is praise. My glory, really, is God's glory.

Makes sense, I think, and helps us see an even more human King David.

Lord, some passages in the Bible—like Psalm 4—seem to lack rhythm or clarity. But thank you for the revelation that's always there, even outside the words—that you love your people, and that you sent your Son to save us. Amen.

POLITICS

"The LORD sustains the humble but casts
the wicked to the ground."
—Psalm 147:6

Over the years, some people have claimed that religion would someday fade away. Think of Harvey Cox's best-seller, *The Secular City,* once a classic, or *Time* magazine's much ballyhooed cover story, forty years ago, proclaiming the death of God. Or think of John Lennon, who once famously remarked that the Beatles were more popular than Jesus. He's been dead and gone for thirty years now.

Recently Elton John, the British pop star, said there would be no religion in his world. "Organised religion doesn't seem to work. It turns people into really hateful lemmings and it's not really compassionate," he told a magazine reporter.

But in my lifetime at least, faith—and its organized work force, religion—has never played such a prominent and fearful role in the world.

There must be a hundred reasons or more for the permanence of faith in the human psyche, but certainly one of them is the undeniable political force so clearly manifest in this line from Psalm 147: "The LORD sustains the humble but casts the wicked to the ground." That line promises to all who are dispossessed a glorious regime change.

In the last century, the number of Christians in Africa rose from just under 10 percent to the neighborhood of half the population. By 2025, researchers predict that half the Christians in the world will live in Africa and Latin America; 17 percent more will live in Asia. Pentecostalism has grown to 400 million adherents, many of them south of the equator. And in just twenty-five years there will be more Pentecostals, worldwide, than Buddhists.

It's easy for Christians to say that the Holy Spirit is alive and kicking throughout what we used to call the Third World. And it's true.

But some very understandable reasons for this amazing phenomenon exist—and one of them is political. Where there is poverty and injustice, the promise of Psalm 147:6 reads in a radically different way than it does here in my spacious basement office in Sioux Center, Iowa. My enemies aren't easy to locate or to name—but if I were living in Darfur, I wouldn't have to scratch my head to put a finger on "the wicked."

The pledge of Psalm 147:6 is sure: the bad guys will get theirs. Soon enough they'll be six feet under, but the humble—those God loves—will live forever. The spiritual fortitude of that promise is undeniable, but its political dimension is an offer, it seems, to all believers.

It's a huge umbrella really, this pledge of happiness and the end of sorrow, bigger than I ever thought it was when I was younger, when I was more idealistic—and more combative. People read it in a hundred different ways, and more.

I've never done the math, but it seems to me that no single promise is more often repeated in the pages of Scripture than this one—God loves the humble. He blesses those on their knees. He stoops to conquer. He will lift the lowly.

That's the song the psalmist sings here in verse 6. And the echo is endless.

⊰⊱✕⊰⊱

Keep us humble, Lord. Remind us of our affluence, our power, the reach of our own arms. Keep us mindful of your favor to those who spend quality time on their knees. Refresh us with your immensity so we know our finite selves. Amen.

THE BEAUTY OF THE LORD

"May the favor of the Lord our God rest on us. . . ."
—Psalm 90:17

One of my grandmother's older sisters had had a very difficult life in the early years of the twentieth century. She'd had but two children, one of whom died as a child—I don't know why, and neither does anyone else, a century later. Grandma's sister's name was Cora, and her husband was a salesman. One day, Cora's husband simply never returned from work; he left his wife and only child.

Her surviving daughter went off to college—unusual for that time, but then Cora's father was a professor. At college the daughter fell in love with a bright young man with a distinguished academic future. The two of them planned marriage, once he could get a job and they could get themselves financially stable. Then Cora's daughter, soon to be a bride, came down with a strange disease. Soon she died, leaving Cora all alone.

I heard that story from an aunt, who remembered being told as a child.

There's more. Some time later, Cora died. And when her relatives looked through her belongings—there were no heirs and no spouse— they found a letter in her desk addressed to the husband who'd abandoned her, a letter Cora had written, knowing that someday she would die and hoping that something of hers would find its way to him, wherever he might be.

That letter, my aunt told me, explained that she loved him so much that, after he left, every night she'd stay awake until, finally, she'd hear the wheels of the last Wealthy Street trolley move slowly away into the night.

91

That sound of those wheels stays with me, carrying the portrait of an abandoned wife who has buried her only two children, a woman who waits every night, hoping to hear footsteps coming up the sidewalk to the front door of her empty home.

My aunt told that story for another reason — she wanted to describe my grandmother, a woman I never knew.

Because there is still more. On the walls of my grandmother's bedroom, she kept a collection of pictures of her family, including a snapshot of her sister, Cora, with two small children. When Grandma was dying, and suffering — according to the aunt who told me this — she looked across the room and saw that picture, then asked if someone would please turn it away from her. The very sight of her sister Cora brought back the pain of a story that, even on her own deathbed, broke her heart.

Some other Bible versions translate Psalm 90:17 this way: "May the *beauty* of the Lord shine upon us." I don't doubt for a moment that that's what my grandmother wanted, especially on her deathbed — only the beauty of the Lord. Clearly it's what Moses wanted — not only for himself, but for his people. Psalm 90 rises in his parched soul from far too many Aunt Cora stories out there in the desert.

Grandma wanted it, and so did Moses — the beauty of the Lord shining upon them. Don't we all?

Some of the radiance of God's divine beauty is already here, even in the forbidding darkness of this great psalm from the soul of Moses. It's here. Go ahead, read the whole thing.

Thank you for the great gift of Psalm 90, the testimony of a man who had seen so much in his life, such miracles, such devotion — but also such rancor and rebellion. Thank you for Moses, in whom we find ourselves and our own ways — and for his testimony. Thank you for faithfulness. Keep us faithful. Amen.

MY CUP OVERFLOWS

"You anoint my head with oil; my cup overflows."
—Psalm 23:5

Not long ago on a Sunday morning, I called my mother. She lives in a retirement home—it's beautiful and spacious, but I'm deeply struck, every time I visit, with the depth of its silence. At meal times people gather on the first floor, as some do each morning for exercise; but otherwise the dark and thickly carpeted hallways are eerily quiet. So much of the world, outside the walls of that home, doesn't register.

Mom said she was doing as well as could be expected, the usual pains and burdens, and, occasionally, usually at night, more than a little loneliness since my father's death. Otherwise, things were fine. The food—yeah, well, it could be better, but she has her own stove and refrigerator for times the menu looks less than appealing.

Yesterday morning, she said, her friend Ed didn't show up, and it seemed strange to be missing him at breakfast. Then another resident told her Ed had died the night before, a heart attack probably. Whoever came in to take care of his passing had deliberately avoided disturbing the silence. It was, after all, the middle of the night.

"Well," she told me, "things like that happen in the world I live in."

She's right, of course, not only of her world, but ours. But then, few of us outside those walls awaken so frequently to significantly altered breakfast tables.

"Did you hear Dr. Martin this morning?" she asks, assuming we're as earnest as she is about TV ministries. "I just love him," she says. "His messages always bring such a blessing—and Taylor, did you catch his sermon? What a joy that was, huh?"

I'm truly thankful for those pastors (I don't remember their real names). I'm thankful the Lord uses them and a host of others to channel the Holy Spirit into a room my mom occupies alone. And I'm thankful—and amazed—at my mother's joy.

It's my granddaughter's fourth birthday today. Yesterday, she and her mother made special cupcakes—white frosting—for all the kids at day care. Today there will be presents galore. Her cup will overflow when she sits in front of her cake and blows out the candles. It's not quite seven in the morning right now. But I'm betting that, somewhere across town, she's already up and tooling around in her pj's.

Would that we all were as easy to please as my granddaughter and her great-grandmother, and as David must have been when he first sang this most famous of his songs!

My granddaughter's joy is far less difficult for me to understand. In the confines of her world, darling little cupcakes may well be all she needs to overflow.

My mother's joy is more inspiring, perhaps because it's harder for me to imagine. I've not yet come to that point in my life when friends suddenly stop showing up for breakfast.

King David sings because he knows he's loved by God almighty. And his song echoes through the centuries because so many millions of us know that too—my granddaughter, for one, and my mother, for another.

It is a special gift of God to be able to recognize grace for the journey, whether God's love comes by way of white frosting on cupcakes or TV preachers in the silence of a retirement home. To be blessed is to know how richly our cups overflow.

For some of us, counting blessings is a huge task. Chalking up credit to God for the good, good things is almost too big a job! Give us grace to recognize our blessings as gifts from the Lord God almighty, King of heaven and earth. Make our hearts sing at the way our cups overflow. Amen.

SURROUND SOUND

*"But the LORD's unfailing love surrounds
those who trust in him."*
—Psalm 32:10

Our preacher once said that the first words the angel chorus offered the quaking shepherds on the hills of Galilee are the entire Scripture in a nutshell. "Fear not," they said to those miscreant stargazers. And that is, in a way, the whole Word of the Lord to those who love him: "Fear not."

Those words are the heart and soul of this verse too, as well as the answer to the first question of the catechism I was raised on—"What is your only comfort in life and in death?" "That I am not my own, but belong—body and soul, in life and in death—to my faithful Savior Jesus Christ." Same thing.

"The Lord's unfailing love surrounds the man who trusts in him," says Psalm 32:10. *Surrounds*. When my grandson and I go to the park a couple of blocks from our house, he's a terror. He'll try anything. The only way for me to keep him from scoring something purple on his forehead is to stand beside him or around him or behind him, close enough so that at any moment I can save him from his own . . . what? His own silliness, childishness, inexperience, innocence? Maybe I should say, save him from being a child. Not unlike us.

That may not be exactly what the verse implies, perhaps, but it's close. Try this—God's love makes us all look like the Michelin Man. OK, maybe that's not the best image. Those rubber suits might get a little cumbersome, and tap dancing would definitely be a problem.

How about this one? When we trust God, we're perfectly outfitted with airbags. That is, *surrounded*. Somehow that doesn't quite ring true either—people get whacked by airbags.

The first time I turned on our kids' DVD player and heard the sound of *Tora, Tora, Tora*—or whatever—through speakers mounted in every corner of the room, the soundtrack nearly took my breath away. I felt as if I was in the middle of the action. God's love is like surround sound. It's all over.

We are cocooned by God's favor, swaddled in his love. Whatever happens, we're in his hands—always, forever.

Am I getting there? Maybe.

If you think I'm being glib, you may be right. I'm sitting here smiling, but the implication of this verse is so good that it's tough not to be a little flighty. It's hard to write without a smile.

Now let me get serious.

Two weeks ago, a woman told me how, one night here on the prairie, her husband and young son were killed by a tornado that left her hospitalized, left her on the edge of death and despair. The only thing that got her through her travail, she told me, was her repetition of the answer I quoted above: "I am not my own. I am not my own, but belong—body and soul, in life and in death—to my faithful Savior Jesus Christ. . . . I am not my own."

In life and in death, David says, fear not. The love of God surrounds you unfailingly. Say it again and again, Michelin Man.

⚜———⚜

Nobody's life escapes the blues, Lord. Suffering is everywhere. Still, what comfort it is to know that you care, that you're always there, surrounding us like nothing else. Thank you for your love. Amen.

THE HOUSE OF THE LORD

"... and I will dwell in the house of the LORD forever."
—Psalm 23:6

"In any story by Edgar Allan Poe," someone once said, "no one ever eats breakfast."

What this person meant is that Poe's characters aren't really supposed to be human. Poe loved characters and worlds that didn't exist, perhaps in part because he found this one so very difficult.

I've never been a big Poe fan, but one aspect of his stories I find really appealing—even though you might call it silly. If you look closely at some of Poe's stories—"The Fall of the House of Usher," for instance—the physical house itself, the very walls, seem to breathe, to have their own life. They're hardly inanimate.

Last night I drove through the pick-up lane at Hardee's in the neighborhood where we used to live. I saw once again the upstairs window I used to look out of when putting our baby son to sleep. The floor plan of that home will never leave me. On the east side, upstairs, my little daughter used to sleep beneath windows where dawn turned the whole world glorious. In the room between, my wife and I shared intimacies that seem now almost furtive, between our two little kids.

In the basement southeast corner, on a floor covered with secondhand rugs I continuously replaced after heavy spring rains, I wrote a few books. One of them paid for the furnace, the one that replaced the old oil burner. There's a wall-sized book rack we made in the family room, and in one of my short stories there's a description of the way the January sun used to slant through the windows of the living room.

I don't know who lives there now. But whoever it is knows nothing about the life the Schaap family invested in that place, our first Iowa home. Maybe that's why I like Poe's living houses with their walls that seem to pulsate. Maybe those walls have memories. But then, his houses, like his characters, never eat breakfast.

Any story of King David's life has to include his lifelong passion for building the house of the Lord, his burning desire to create an intimate space for God. But that was not to be. The Lord God didn't want David's hands on the tools. "You are a man of war and have shed blood," God told him.

That passion—and the rejection—is part of the baggage of this famous last line of this famous psalm. Here's a man who couldn't do what he wanted to. His resolution is the stronger for having been once forbidden.

And that makes the "forever"-ness of this verse so memorable. King David's heart nearly explodes when he testifies here that he's not going to move, he's not going to leave anything behind. There will be no history, only the present in this forever house of the Lord, the one he's wanted for so long. "That's where I'm going to be," says the rejected builder, "and that's where I'm going to live forever."

See him pointing? And he's smiling. Forever.

What a story! What a believer!

***

This world is not our home, Lord—we're just passing through. That reality is unmistakable. But help us to love it, not abandon it. Help us to cherish our lives, even as we've got our eyes on the prize of eternity. Amen.

HARMONY

"I will praise you, Lord, among the nations;
I will sing of you among the peoples."
—Psalm 57:9

I have but two memories of an early childhood trip to New York City, and both of them emerge from adroit fear.

I had to be younger than ten. We visited the United Nations, because I have some kind of memory of standing in front of that building, but no memories at all of being inside.

What I remember best, as I said, is two images, both from the street. In one, a woman who is apparently mad is screaming wildly. The words make no sense, as I remember; but the scene is distressing, largely because no one seems to care. People—hundreds of them—walk right past her on sidewalks wider than I'd ever seen in my life. *Someone should tell her not to scream, because it's so disturbing*, I thought. But no one did, and she kept it up. Finally we were out of earshot.

The other image is of a man in a sandwich board saying, "Repent." I was a kid, but I remember being embarrassed, almost the same feeling I had when that madwoman wouldn't stop screaming. This guy was preaching, and I knew it, but I found it embarrassing, even repulsive. I didn't want him drawing attention to something I knew better by the warmth of Christmas Eve programs or the comfort of morning prayers over Sugar Pops.

Those two memories are filed away in a similar folder or scrapbook — the most vivid memories of a child's first trip to the big city.

Gratitude is the beginning of the Christian life—that's what I believe—and gratitude makes us sing. No question. Gratitude makes David pipe the dawn in this psalm, or believe he can—or at least make the outrageous claims. Our thanks for the salvation that has come so shockingly into our lives sends us all cart-wheeling into the world. "I will sing of you among the peoples," David shouts, ecstatic. And some guy in early 1950s New York adorns himself in sandwich boards, standing out on the street, where he scares children and horses.

Our pastor tells of a young man with Down syndrome in a previous congregation who had a special love for a certain organist's playing. Whenever she'd play, he'd dance in the aisles.

Maybe we all should. Maybe we all should pull on a sandwich board or paint "Jesus loves me" across the side of our houses. There's a man just down the block that loves to sit outside on Sunday afternoons, his stereo cranked, the sounds of "The Old Rugged Cross" sung by a men's quartet with bluegrass roots taking over the entire neighborhood.

I know the impulse of this line. David is almost gone in his deep affection for the God who has saved him so often and here, in the cave, God has done it again. God's delivered him, and it's as obvious as the nose on his face that David's going to sing about it.

But what song? What tune? How loud? Snare drums or flutes? Bold type or italics? Stories or poems? Classical or folk rock? Johnny Cash or Mahalia Jackson? Flannery O'Connor or Robert Schuller?

The older I get, the more I think the answer is simply, "Just sing." Sing and let God do the harmony.

When we want to sing our gratitude, Lord, show us the notes. Screaming on street corners may not be the best way to pass along the peace of your love, but don't allow us to stop dancing once in awhile. Make us fine singers. We've already got the music. Amen.

HALLELUJAH

"Praise the LORD, my soul. Praise the LORD."
—Psalm 104:35

Tomorrow night, I'm going to a book club. We'll discuss *March* by Geraldine Brooks, but my estimate of the book won't change—I liked it. Our discussion will hold few surprises.

The truth is, I'd rather be playing slo-pitch. A math professor, older than I am, decided the college faculty should have an intramural softball team. He called his team the Geezers. He organized it, and now he's got them out on the field. They got thumped in their first game, so the coach sent out an e mail looking for beefier hitters. Singles just don't make it in slo-pitch.

I used to slam homers methodically, routinely—every other at bat, almost. No lie. The siren call of playing slo-pitch got even sweeter when the Geezers took it on the chin from a bunch of squirt students who pounded home runs like pop flies.

But I can't go play slo-pitch. One reason is the book club. Another is that I'm just getting too old. I don't like to think about what might happen to this body should I throw hard, swing hard, or even run, for that matter. This mortal coil has experienced nothing close to any of the above for more than a decade. Who knows what horrors I'd inflict?

No matter—if I weren't at the book club, I'd be at the ball diamond. I would. I swear. At least I think so.

A friend of mine remembers the day his father, seventy-plus, looked at him sardonically when this friend complained of some minor muscle ache. "Get used to it," he said, with far more authority than sympathy.

Most mornings when I wake, I walk downstairs slowly, the railing in my right hand, my left braced up against the wall, my back crooked, knees only half unfurled. My silhouette against the dim kitchen lights must resemble Notre Dame's famous hunchback. And it ain't getting better.

I wash small loads of wash lately, more often than I'd like to admit, because once a week at least a perfectly clean shirt jumps off my chest to catch milk from the cereal bowl or syrup from pancakes. I wash them right away to destroy the evidence.

But this friend of mine—the man who was warned by his father to get used to his aches and pains—right now, my friend is dying of lung cancer. A note he sent me says that his aches are different because now: "I will never again be able to draw a full two lungs' worth of breath. I will never puff at a flight of stairs. This body will never more be what it has been, nor can I frame my knowing it according to its ability to repair itself."

He'll never get better, he says. He's busy "devising methods for living the diminishing life." And still he says, "Praise the Lord." He still says, "Hallelujah." Just doesn't have as much lung power to propel the praise.

I'd like to think I could still hit a ball out of the park, but I'm a whole lot safer at the book club. And I hope that, like my friend, when my time comes I can call upon an ever-youthful faith and say with the psalmist at the very end of this psalm, "Hallelujah, praise the Lord."

⊱✕⊰

Some folks get cynical. They lose their sense of humor. Their passion for life itself goes cold. Keep me from losing the joy of the psalmist, Lord. Keep me from being unable to sing for joy, even in these later years. Amen.

BLESSED

"Blessed are those whose transgressions are forgiven. . . ."
— Psalm 32:1

The word *blessed* — and what it suggests — is a treasure. And you don't have to believe in Jesus Christ's redemptive work to aspire to the riches the word suggests. I doubt anyone's ever done a poll, but my guess is that most of those who spend their nights at what America calls "gaming" would embrace the word as lovingly as I do. Seated in front of slots or at the poker table, they too would love to be *blessed*, in their case by what they'd call luck.

I believe that everyone — from Pope Benedict XVI to last week's serial killer — wants, more than anything, to be "blessed." I know I do. A considerable number of us, like Jacob, would even fake IDs to get it, if we sensed we were in the neighborhood. To be blessed is a pursuit that dominates our dreams.

Just a few weeks ago, we buried a man named Henry. He was devout but never, ever self-righteous, always courteous and loving and considerate. I visited him in the hospital when his wife of sixty years was close to death, very close. He spoke to her and read to her, even smiled at her as if she hung on his every word. Maybe she did, but I doubt it.

If those who knew him best ever saw another side of Henry, I don't want to know. But I'm enough of a Calvinist to believe he was probably capable of something other than the grace that radiated from his presence as long as I knew him. I'm sure he wrestled with his own inner demons, fought his own battles.

When Henry knew his own death was imminent, he wrote a note to his children that all the travel costs his geographically-dispersed family would incur for his funeral should be paid before anyone looked into his estate. By profession, he'd been a professor of business; that little note was scribbled by the accountant in him. But it was also the act of a man who knew he'd been blessed and understood that his role was to do likewise.

I bring him up only because it seems to me that, through our lives, most of us know very, very few people to whom we might affix the description of being truly blessed. Henry was one of those. I'm blessed—as all of us were in this community—to have known him.

So how do we go about getting blessed? Is there something we can do, or is it simply a gift, like grace itself?

Psalm 1 begins with the same word as does Psalm 32, but then it describes the condition of being blessed by illustrating how the blessed among us conduct their lives, what they do and don't do. Psalm 32, on the other hand, is more of a how-to, a sermon psalm.

So read on for yourself. Consider its ways and be wise. Consider its ways and be *blessed*. Follow the instructions, if indeed you can.

Lord, only the deranged desire something other than to be happy. The rest of us—believers and non-believers included—simply want to be blessed. But none are blessed like those who trust in you and know the grace of Christ. Thank you for the greatest gift anyone can receive. In your Son's name, amen.

LIFE AND DEATH

"... When you take away their breath, they die and
return to the dust. When you send your Spirit,
they are created, and you renew the face of the ground."
—Psalm 104:29-30

On Thursday, the classroom was overheated. As the afternoon sun poured in through the windows, the heat felt like a wall. "Let's go outside," kids said. In a couple of minutes we were seated in green grass beneath the outstretched arms of a massive maple. I talked too much, as old teachers do—as I do anyway—and when it was over I told myself the hour and a half probably seemed to my students little more than words.

Then I got an e-mail from Sarah. "I hope you are having a good day!" it said. "I greatly enjoyed your lecture today. It was wonderful to sit outside."

I felt like teacher of the year.

Even though all of us have an infinite need to be loved, that insatiable appetite can be satisfied with two skinny lines in an e-mail. So very little.

A week ago, my wife took her mother off to a regional hospital for a surgery that didn't happen—her mother's condition was too fragile. Today, we count what remains of her life in teaspoons, day by day. Her mother would much rather that her life was over. Every day, we simply wait and pray.

That very same morning, at the very same moment, our daughter was up early, holding back tears because her daughter, her first child—was going off to her first day of kindergarten.

On one clear morning last week, we felt the ominous heft of last rites and the cheerful blessing of first things. Such is life.

Yesterday two precious letters arrived. One was from the aging parents of a woman who died of ovarian cancer, a woman I helped by arranging her journals into a narrative of her dying. They were very thankful for her book, they said. We keep it beside the couch, they wrote, in spidery handwritten lines, and we pick it up often during the day.

The other letter asked for photographs. It came from a woman whose husband, a wonderful and much-beloved writer, is dying of lung cancer. "Could you send some 8 x 10s?" she asked. "The cards you sent with those pictures of the dawn have been such blessings to us."

I'll do it today.

Last night, my wife and I went out on a date—a ritual of sorts—barbeque ribs at a joint across the river. On the drive home, a deer stopped along the road, looked at us for a moment, then loped off through a field of gorgeous yellowing soybeans. When we came home, we made love.

Life is so precious, its joys so brittle, so sweet—a few good words, a dawn, a little barbeque sauce, an acquaintance with a deer, cherished flesh shared, and all of it made more precious, surely, by the imminent reality of dying.

All of which is, by my reckoning at least, the subject of Psalm 104. Our lives are precarious, and they are in God's hands. He owns our breath. He's the God of collapsed veins and kindergartens, of overheated rooms and postal delivery. To God belong our moments of death and the joys of our lives. That's what Psalm 104 says.

---

*Give us the wisdom to number our days, to enjoy time itself,
a wonderful gift. Give us the depth of soul to see beauty in
an owl's midnight call, the swaying arms of an old maple
on a warm fall afternoon. Give us vision, Lord.
In your Son's name, amen.*

WOUNDS

"[The LORD] heals the brokenhearted
and binds up their wounds."
—*Psalm 147:3*

Our newspaper cunningly stopped placing free obituaries a few years ago; today, obits are paid columns; almost daily, those notices spread over two whole pages of the front news section. Even though no one has ever escaped it, death is still news.

Some deaths are more so than others. Soon my wife's mother will pass away. For her, it can't be soon enough. She has no mobility and very little sight, and she feels constant dizziness. When she goes, we'll ache; but there will be precious few at her funeral, and other than the effect on her husband and my wife, she will leave this world almost seamlessly.

I remember a few tragic accidents of my boyhood, and children lost to friends. I wasn't at my father's bedside when he died, but I was there for hours before the night he finally succumbed. I've not been the same since.

In the town where I live, the death I'll not forget is the passing of a high school senior who fell to a mysterious killer that took her slowly, while all around her hundreds of thousands of prayers rose daily. A teacher at the Christian school she attended told me it was the worst semester he'd ever spent in education because the kids—unaccustomed to death and drawn like moths to the flame of deep emotion—simply couldn't study. Their friend was dying, and no one—not even God almighty—seemed able to lift a finger.

Finally, months after first feeling something akin to flu symptoms, she fell to that mysterious disease—mercifully, I suppose. What once seemed beyond belief became, well, inexorable. But it took months.

Imagine the endless, fervent prayers of hundreds of high school classmates. Imagine the minds, hearts, and souls of her parents.

One of the most difficult lessons we learn is that sometimes God doesn't seem to answer our prayers, no matter how often we pound on his door or how arduously we beg. Sometimes we just don't get what we want.

That high school senior's parents worship beside us every Sunday. They carry wounds whose flow of grief in the last decade hasn't been totally stanched. The death of their daughter must rise from the broad plains of their many years together like some black obelisk of cut glass. It will always be that way—until the day each of them is gone.

Life in that high school has returned to normal. Talking about what happened a decade ago would be like a history lesson. A few staff remember. There may be a picture of her on a wall, but few students have any idea about her story.

Believers like me live in the assurance that assertions like this one— that the Lord "heals the brokenhearted"—isn't just cheerleading, even though we know mysterious killers stalk the countryside. Faith consents to the illogical assertion that somehow God will be there, even when he seems to be out of the building.

Faith believes that the Lord will heal, that he will, forever and ever, bind up our wounds. Faith sinks its teeth in and tries to hold on.

Be a presence to those who think you're absent today—and there are many. Come into their homes and shine, Lord. Don't let people who love you feel abandoned. Strengthen them, wherever they are, with your love. Amen.

PERFECT IN BEAUTY

"From Zion, perfect in beauty, God shines forth."
—Psalm 50:2

Last night, after shoveling snow for the first time this winter—not an easy job because of the rain that fell before the storm—I put the shovel back in the garage and stood out back for a moment in the semidarkness. Winter had come; the world was white.

We're three blocks, max, from Main Street—far too close at this time of year because the mini-mall downtown pipes Christmas Muzak all over the parking lot and consequently all over the surrounding neighborhood. We hear it whether we want to or not. Fortunately, our windows are shut tight or "White Christmas" would find its way inside like those pesky Asian beetles that just now are dying thanks to the cold.

I love Christmas music. I must have been part of a thousand gatherings where "Joy to the World" brings the assembled to their feet, and I never tire of it. "Lo, How a Rose E'er Blooming" is as gorgeous as it is haunting, and the refrain of "Hark, the Herald Angels Sing" conjures up all the very best images of all my Christmases past. My wife and I rarely play anything on the old music center in the living room. But a week before Christmas, Handel's *Messiah* is on most of the time.

I'm no Scrooge, is what I'm saying, but I find the mall's constant blaring of seasonal music horribly annoying.

Christmas itself is so familiar, so intimate, that it seems almost like a spouse, or maybe a sibling from whom we expect so much that we can't help but somehow get let down. Yuletide brings out the best in us—and the worst. A whole lot of us have a love/hate thing with the whole season. Ask any crisis center. Suicides jump in the middle of all that caroling.

But having said that, and despite the Wal-Mart excesses of Black Friday, the whole season is an immense blessing for all of us—no matter what our faith.

I'm still happy for the season. I love the golden glow our huge wreath casts nightly over the snow down the alley. I love the hand-carved nativity scene that comes out of nowhere and sits on our magazine table. I love the tree decorations, little tokens of where we've been throughout our married life. I love buying gifts for people, lots of them—little things, red licorice for my wife. I love the story. I love the love he's brought—Jesus Christ that is. At Christmas, we're all kids.

I'm not sure I can recapture what the psalmist sees in Psalm 50:2, because in that writer's mind, God almighty actually lived in the temple. I don't have any pictures for what he meant by God "shining forth" from Zion.

The closest I can come is Christmas because what happens throughout the world, the *whole* world, not just the Christian world, at Christmas is an immense blessing. At Christmas, God's perfect beauty shines forth, sometimes in very imperfect ways. And what it brings is, well, joy to the world.

Thank you for coming into the world, Lord, not to condemn it but to save it. Thank you for the innocence of the baby, the cattle lowing, the mother and father adoring. Thank you for taking on our flesh and blood, dear Jesus. Amen.

HELP

"I lift up my eyes to the mountains —
where does my help come from?"
—Psalm 121:1

I wasn't sure where my daughter's question came from, and I was busy thinking of something else at the time. That's why I didn't give her a very good answer, not a fatherly answer anyway.

"When you were my age," she said, sort of laughing, "did you ever think that the world was just going to come to an end?"

My daughter is thirty. When I was that age, my wife and I had her. But right then I couldn't remember ever thinking the world was in imminent danger of coming to an end. I smiled and said no, rolled my eyes, and turned back to the computer screen.

Later, I couldn't sleep.

I was a kid, but I remember learning to crawl under my school desk should nuclear holocaust come to Oostburg, Wisconsin. I grew up in the Cold War, when the Soviets were capable of pushing the wrong button or pushing the right one wrongly.

I remember walking on a football field during the Cuban missile crisis and having a profound talk with a kid about whether or not we'd ever have a season. We both knew football was a metaphor; we were talking about the end of the world.

I remember the comet Kohoutek and Y2K. I remember a number of primitive eschatologies — Hal Lindsey's *Late Great Planet Earth*, for instance — that ordered our days by manipulating ancient calendars suggested in the minor prophets. End-times theology is big business today, everybody and their dog wanting not to be Left Behind.

I believe my daughter's generation lives in more fear than mine did because I was reared with more freedom than her kids will ever see. When I was ten, my friends and I took our bikes down to Lake Michigan and lost ourselves and our inhibitions in endless woods. Today that land is private property; and today, no parent would allow her ten-year-old kid that kind of freedom.

The parade of prospective students will start any day now at the college where I teach, and with them come loving, helicopter parents, moms and dads who ask more questions about college than their children do. I never visited the college where I enrolled. My parents drove me there — 500 miles — then left. That was it.

As I write, a congressional election looms. The war in Iraq isn't going well. Even the President wishes we were no longer there, I'm sure. But in order to keep his party in office, he and other Republicans are making sure the American people know that the Democrats, should they win, will cut and run; when they do, the Islamic extremists will terrorize us, even here in a woebegone corner of the rural Midwest. Fear sells.

So this is a better answer than my eye-rolling, Andrea: Yes, I've felt that way. We all have. We've all been afraid. Even the psalmist.

While the psalms tell us bountifully about God, they're even better at telling us about ourselves. We're not alone — in more ways than one.

⤜✕⤛

Calm our fears and anxiousness, Lord. We're wealthier than we've ever been, but we're probably also more afraid. The light seems full of darkness, oddly enough. Infuse us with the quiet strength of your promises. Amen.

A PILGRIMAGE

"Blessed are those whose strength is in you,
whose hearts are set on pilgrimage."
—*Psalm 84:5*

Today my wife and I will go to a wedding rehearsal. Two kids I met just yesterday will exchange vows, and I'm conducting the ceremony. I'm not ordained. The couple's uncle is a judge; he'll make the bond legal. They wanted someone to "do the wedding." I've never "done a wedding," but this is family, not close family, but family.

I admire their idealism, even their estimable foolhardiness in simply tying the knot. Getting married is a good thing, the right thing to do, even if this second cousin is likely to fumble through the proceedings. In Protestant tradition marriage is not a sacrament; but, Lord knows, it is a big deal.

I'm of an age when this couple's sweet resolve to plunge into a legal and binding contract, seems, well, dreamy in an adolescent way. The whole thing seems scary. They are so young. They've been dating seven years, which has a somewhat biblical sound. But face it: they don't know squat.

In their mid-eighties, my parents suddenly turned into scrappers, even though I don't remember their ever being particularly cross with each other before, at least in my presence. They got in each others' hair something awful. Sometimes it was funny; mostly sad. In the end, do we really go it alone, like the medieval play *Everyman* promises? Do even our closest relationships skip out? I suppose so.

What I know is this. Last night my wife and I skipped an end-of-year gala and stayed home by ourselves, in part because we're becoming less social, but also because in our thirty-five-year marriage, right now nothing seems more blessed than being alone, just the two of us. Playing hooky on a gala was low-stakes. Couch potatoes get bad press.

I could try to explain all of that to this young couple—I've got to give a homily; I could tell them how we stayed home and simply enjoyed each other. I could try, but their being twenty-two means they wouldn't begin to understand.

They've got their own pilgrimage ahead, just as we did, and our parents before us. All the diagrams, the how-to's, all the counseling sessions we could offer will mean little to them because they'll have to create their own map as they go, just as we did.

Every cow-eyed young couple carries our hopes with them when they recite their vows; because our hope, like theirs, is for nothing less than the very first word of Psalm 84:5—to be *blessed*.

I cannot imagine life without faith. Faith was the soul of our solitary night together, even though we didn't recite Bible verses. The two of us have spent hours and hours in prayer in the last two years, hours of pleading that sometimes seem fruitless. But we'll keep praying because faith isn't something one wears like a tux; and we are blessed—as the psalmist says—by putting our faith in God. I know that's true. Our pilgrimage, begun so long ago, continues.

I hope somewhere down the line we don't start to carp at each other; but then, my mother would roll her eyes if I brought up the subject. "What do you know, really, about *pilgrimage*, young as you are?" she'd say. And she'd probably be right.

What she'd tell me, unequivocally, is that her sixty years of marriage was a great ride, a pilgrimage, begun and lived in faith. She'd say, I'm sure, she was blessed.

Bless that young couple and all those who are making commitments to stay together for a lifetime, bound together in their mutual confession of their love for each other and for you. And be with those too who don't have faith and still commit. Bless them—as you've blessed us. Amen.

WRATH

"If only we knew the power of your anger!
Your wrath is as great as the fear that is your due."
—*Psalm 90:11*

I'm going to make a generalization here. One of the good things about aging is that, through the years, we grow less angry—Jack Lemmon, Walter Matthau, and *Grumpy Old Men* notwithstanding. Old bucks like me simply have less testosterone to work with, less dignity to protect, less turf to maintain—thus, fewer reasons to boil over.

When so many things recede the way they do as we get older, quarrelsomeness is a possibility—I'll grant you that. Fewer people notice us—again, my perception. But that doesn't make me mad, just bad-tempered. Being peevish isn't the same thing as being wrathful.

But last night I was mad. Last night, I used language I shouldn't have, even to my daughter, who didn't have it coming, who had nothing to do with why I was boiling over. Last night—memorably, I might add—I was spitting fire.

This morning I could still throw flames; in fact, I sent out an e-mail I probably shouldn't have. But I've calmed down now, a bit; and having that rare chunk of lava-rage at arm's length this morning is helpful when reading this strange verse from Psalm 90. It's helpful because normally it's easy for me to get a little embarrassed by the Old Testament's occasionally draconian Jehovah. I find it hard to know him, maybe in part because I don't know all that much anymore about rage. Wrath isn't the deadly sin I register all that often.

But I did last night. What blew my cork was that I didn't get my way. We'd worked our duffs off, but our whole project shipwrecked because someone in authority thought *maybe* someone else might be hurt. Honestly, the whole story is not worth a story.

But maybe my wrath is worth a story when I think about this line from the venerable Psalm 90. Here's what I'm thinking: Maybe the Old Testament God isn't a far cry from who I am. The whole Exodus narrative suggests that what God wants more than anything is not to be an also-ran. In the panoply of gods available to the Israelites, he doesn't want to be just another graven image.

"Who should I say this God is?" Moses—the writer here—asks. "I am the always," God says. End of story. And when he isn't respected—when people create golden calves of whatever size and extremity—this God, Jehovah, spits and fumes. And often enough, people die. He's like me that way. Sort of. I'm human. He's not. And nobody died last night.

Oddly enough, maybe I don't think of God as human enough. If I were him and people didn't really give me the dignity I'd deserved, I'd be mad—like I was last night. Maybe all that anger, behind me now, maybe even all that blasted wrath was helpful. You think you got dissed?—just think of God. And on a daily basis. Shoot, hourly. Starting right here—with me.

And that's only half of it, this verse says. That's not even the whole story. Your wrath is everything we can imagine, Lord—that's what Moses says.

If only we knew!

⤜✕⤛

God, you are both not us and not unlike us. We get angry—
you get angry. We love—you love. We fume—you fume.
But you're God, the creator of the universe's myriad black
holes. You bowled the sun into the heavens. You own the
deepest oceans and know who frolics there. Thank you for
your Son, who gave us the best picture of the Father we will
ever see. May we be more like him—and you. Amen.

UNDERSTANDING

"Great is our Lord and mighty in power;
his understanding has no limit."
—Psalm 147:5

I just emptied my trash. Three hundred e-mails, and, with nothing more than a keystroke, they're history, the words simply gone, as if they'd never existed.

Where do they go?—that's what I'm wondering. Isn't there some law of physics that matter simply doesn't disappear? I suppose those three hundred e-mails had no matter; they were nothing more than electronic impulses of some kind. Even so, they mattered. Some time in the next few days I'll remember something I should have done, try to find some tossed note, and discover it and the horse it rode in on, gone. At one time, they mattered.

But now they've vanished, never to be seen again. Strange.

An old friend called last night. His wife, who's been fighting depression for years, has switched meds. "A scary time," he told us, and I understand. What I don't understand is how a pill can actually change character, alter personality, replace whatever it is that makes us each who we are. That's scary. But it happens all the time.

And why is it that I feel so much, of late, that I'd rather be alone than in the blessed company of other people? Once my wife and I were social. Once we looked forward to weekends because they meant games and gatherings. I still look forward to weekends, but the only frivolity I seek is peace and quiet and solitude. If the skies are clear, the dawn compels on Saturday morning. I go alone. That's the way I like it. Why?

Or this. Yesterday in a crowded shopping mall I read a short story from a new collection, read it almost straight though. I was sitting on a bench near the food court, at the very heart of things. Thousands of people passed me by. I saw few. It was a great story. I loved it. Ten years ago—certainly twenty—I could not have sat there amid the thronging shoppers and focused so intensely on a single short story. What has changed in me, and why?

There's so much I don't understand.

Why do we suffer—honestly? The older I become, the more Job appears, just off my shoulder, one hand raised to heaven in a fist. Three of my friends are dying of cancer; all of them would love to live. None of them are ancient. Yet, all over North America people are building nursing homes to tend the millions who would, any day of the week, volunteer tomorrow for a long-sought trip to glory.

I was born after the Second World War, but I've spent more time reading the literature of the Holocaust than perhaps I should have. *Arbeit macht frei*—there's a sign in my mind that will never leave. I know where Dr. Mengele stood at the platform as the trains rolled into Auschwitz. I can see his hand determining. This way, showers— that way, labor. And even though I wasn't there, I can hear millions of bootless cries to heaven.

I don't understand about life and about death, about suffering and joy. So much mystery.

And the greatest mystery of all is a gift, a sumptuous gift. I don't know why his grace comes to me, but I believe that even though I don't get it, even though this flesh will corrupt and I will die, God knows. His understanding has no limit. Bless his holy name.

⊱⊰

If one of the gifts of aging is silence, Lord, then turn up the volume on the clock's ticking. Help me be still in your presence; let loose my fears, my sadness, my hurt. I know the line—"You are my only comfort." Help me to act that way. Amen.

"LIKE A DAY THAT HAS JUST GONE BY"

"A thousand years in your sight are like a day that has
just gone by, or like a watch in the night."
—*Psalm 90:4*

When my father died, the poet Scott Cairns sent me a poem he'd written at the death of his own father. Like no other poem I know, it offered great consolation—and still does. Countless times I've sent it on to others who've lost parents or friends. It's titled "Words for a Father," and it begins with "and," as if we're probably overhearing some ideas that have been brewing in our own heads for quite some time.

> And this is the consolation: that the world
> doesn't end, that the world one day opens up
> into something better. And that we
> one day open up into something far better.

He's talking about afterlife, of course—our visions of the eternal, of heaven. None of us know a thing about what the afterlife will look like, but our differing views (streets paved with gold, good fishing, no more wind) all share the same basic conviction: Things will be better. That much for sure.

Then he visits a possible vision of things, narrating carefully one possible scenario after dying:

> Maybe like this: one morning you finally wake
> to a light you recognize as the light you've wanted
> every morning that has come before. And the air
> has some light thing in it that you've always hoped

the air might have. And One is there to welcome you
whose face you've looked for during all the best and worst
times of your life. He takes you to himself
and holds you close until you fully wake.

There's no Mormon Tabernacle Choir, only a sweet light and a single, strangely familiar face, a maternal God whose welcome is a blessed, wordless calm.

And then the lines that seem most memorable to me — or certainly *were* in those days following my father's dying.

And it seems you've only just awakened, but you turn
and there we are, the rest of us, arriving just behind you.

We'll go the rest of the way together.

What hurt me most at my father's death was the sense of his being gone, alone, the rest of us seated in the church he'd attended his whole life, all of us, his entire family. To the terror of that emptiness, Scott's poem is sweet and grand relief, profiling eternity by promising us all — my father and his included — that a thousand years in God's sight are like nothing at all. Nothing. We'll be there soon ourselves.

That is comfort.

⧓

None of us know the story of our final chapters, Lord, but all of us who you've claimed in your family know where the story ends — or continues. The end is timelessness, eternity — no more poison ivy, no more bad knees or lower back pain. Bring us home in joy, Lord, as you have loved us before. Amen.

IN HIS FEATHERS

"I will take refuge in the shadow of your
wings until the disaster has passed."
—*Psalm 57:1*

Not long ago I published a collection of a woman's letters and notes and journal entries, which is titled, after this verse, *In His Feathers*. Try as I might, I couldn't find a big publisher—well, let's broaden that a bit: I couldn't find an editor or an agent even willing to read the manuscript.

Why wouldn't anyone take a look? It's the story of one woman's battle with cancer, ovarian cancer. Sharon Wagonaar Bomgaars died in 2003, just a few years after her diagnosis, which means *In His Feathers* is, I suppose, just another memoir by a nobody. If Sharon were a celebrity—say, she'd been featured on *Good Morning America* or *Oprah*—we would have had no trouble finding a publisher.

Sharon was a loving wife and mother, a thoughtful, honest, committed Christian, an inveterate journal-keeper who recorded every last sorrow and joy. Listen to her thoughts as she sat at the keyboard for the very last time:

> This morning [my husband] brought me a half-cup
> of pear juice with ice. I took a sip and a tiny piece
> of pear had slipped through the sieve. I caught it
> on my tongue. I squeezed that little gritty fragment
> lovingly. It smoothed into nothingness and it was so
> good! I squeezed each lovely sip and rolled it around
> on my tongue. Then I let it slide slowly down my
> throat. Pear juice, delicious pear juice, squeezed
> from pears grown on some tree in dusty California,

and now bringing me all its sun-warmed sweetness.
What a gift!

God is so good to give us such pleasures in this sin-
sick world. I love God's gifts! I love his peaches, and
pears, and grapes, and strawberries, and apples!
I love his wet, sweet, juicy creations! What an
awesome God!

Twenty-one days later, she left all those sweet, juicy creations
behind.

Forgive my bitterness and even my jealousy, because I *do* wish the
book would be featured on *Oprah*. But its failure to find a publisher
may well be itself a reason to praise God. Thousands upon thousands
of stories like Sharon's exist, stories of real people who took or take
abiding refuge beneath the wings of God almighty.

The glory and power of this single line from Psalm 57 is that it *is*
true, true until the day we die, and then on into eternity. The proof is
in the numbers: There are so many stories.

Sadly, there's more to Sharon's story. Her husband, just a few years
after Sharon died, was diagnosed with lung cancer even though he
never smoked in his life. Today he's gone too. I'm just happy there's a
book that tells her story, and theirs. It is a love song.

The truth of Sharon's story is in this plaintive song of the poet
king. Refuge, as David knew, even as he sang this line, is under God's
wings and in his feathers.

Thank you for stories that bear witness to your abiding love
and presence, God. Thanks for David's joy here because it
gives us reason to believe that, even in our distress, there's
comfort in your feathers. Amen.

THE LORD'S DELIGHT

"The LORD delights in those who fear him,
who put their hope in his unfailing love."
—*Psalm 147:11*

I t was strange watching the video, eerie. The fire looked rather ordinary, I suppose, an entire chunk of apartment complex going up in flames, smoke everywhere. A helicopter circled the blaze slowly, descending as it did, the camera zooming in close. From east to west, the roof was mostly gone, the whole place a blazing honeycomb.

The last shots of the almost two-minute video were taken quite low. The camera zeroed in on the colonnades of a second-story apartment porch where flames were lapping away at the roof, and something—I couldn't see what—was lying on the cement balcony, in flames.

I could have sworn those final images were our son's apartment.

Yesterday when he called, he started the conversation with a disarming relief: "I'm OK." Then he told me he'd lost almost everything. He had his book bag, his truck, the clothes on his back—and his bike. Everything else—Mac, cell phone, TV and furniture—is gone. All of it.

The Red Cross got him a motel room until Friday when this season's pigskin finale is scheduled and every spare room within a hundred miles of the university is booked. They gave him $100 to buy clothes at Wal-Mart and told him the university would find him a place to live. Others called to offer him a bed. Some woman asked about clothes sizes, and a fraternity was taking up an offering. He hates fraternities—*did* anyway.

He says his cell phone—he bought a new one while the smoke was still rising, and the dealer gave him a $50 credit—has been ringing off the hook, even though, he says, he never gets many calls. It's his first semester at the university.

His parents are not frantic. He's not a child, and I trust the largesse of good people. He won't be alone. So far, he's been shocked himself at the offers of help. They keep coming. I'm sure we'll hear more stories today. Nothing could be better. Nothing.

His parents *are* powerless, however. I would have jumped into the car the moment I put down the phone if he'd asked us to come. But tomorrow he's flying home, as planned.

You wonder why God doesn't see to it that our stuff burns up more often. Maybe this fire has burned up more than our son's earthly goods. Maybe something new will rise from the flames. It has already.

In the last day I've felt closer to the promise of this psalm text than I would have, had you asked, last Wednesday, or Tuesday, or Monday, or even Sunday. In the last twenty-four hours I swear I understand it because I don't know where else to put my trust. God is delighted with my faith, I think, because it's grown not because of anything I did but because I've nowhere else to go with my hope, my trust, my prayers.

Nowhere else to go but the One who delights in our hope because we know his unfailing love—from frat boys and the Red Cross, from friends and strangers. I trust in his love.

About that, God is delighted. And so am I.

❋⤬❋

Lord, right now there are aspects to this unforeseen destruction that make us think there's blessings in all the smoke and haze. We're powerless, but we're reminded again so clearly this day that you aren't. Thank you for surprising us with grace once again. Amen.

BEWONDERMENT

"Be exalted, O God, above the heavens;
let your glory be over all the earth."
—*Psalm 57:5*

The basic paradigm by which I've always seen the Christian life is the outline of a drama that rises from the doctrine with which I was raised. The outline goes like this: Sin, salvation, service.

The story line begins with sin—our knowledge of it as it exists within us. John Calvin starts even a bit earlier, with the heavens, with our sense of God as manifest in his world: what we see and experience. Because humans can't help but see God's marvelous work in the heavens and the earth around us, we come to know that there *is* a God. With that knowledge, we feel our own limitations—we *aren't* God. And so begins our knowledge of human limits, our knowledge, finally, of sin.

That conviction draws us closer to God because we need a Savior. Sin precedes salvation, or so the story goes, through the second act.

Once we know that, in spite of our sin, God loves us, our hearts fill and our souls rejoice. We can't help but celebrate our salvation. That celebration leads us into gratitude and service, that is, acting as God's agents of love in the world he loves so greatly.

Sin, salvation, service—three acts, the narrative by which I was raised.

Mother Teresa's take on a very similar tale in three different acts was shaped, I suppose, by her experiences in the ghettos of Calcutta. Our redemption creates repulsion, she says—what we see offends, prompts us to look away. But we really can't or shouldn't. We have to look misery in its starving face, and when we do, we move from repulsion to compassion—away from rejection and toward loving acceptance. End Act 2.

The final act is what she called *bewonderment*, which is wonder plus admiration. Our compassion leads us to bewonderment.

Bewonderment is one of those words no one uses but everyone understands. It's like *reverence*, hard to come by in a world where, for many of us, our needs are never more than a price tag away.

I'll admit that for me, bewonderment is hard to come by, perhaps because it isn't one of the chapters in the story I was told as a boy, the story that is still deeply embedded in my soul. Service is the end of the Christian life—always has been for me—not bewonderment.

Maybe that's why I'm envious of David's praise here. What he says to God in prayer is something I rarely say. I don't think I've ever asked God *not* to hide his little light under a bushel, to display his radiant grace from pole to pole. I'm forever asking for favors, but only rarely adoring, in part because I'm so rarely in awe.

Bewonderment is something I'm learning, even this morning, and for that I'm thankful—for the book of songs, for David, and for the God David knew so intimately that he could speak the way he did in Psalm 57.

It's difficult for some of us to be intimate with God—so close to a Being so great and grand and seemingly out of reach. But it's something a song can teach—and the heavens too. Even an old man can learn, if he has ears to hear.

⊱✕⊰

Thank you for lessons learned, even if school is almost a lifetime behind us. Thank you for allowing us to be thrilled, to be surprised, to feel bewonderment—and thank you for Mother Teresa and all who teach us how to see. Amen.

HEAVENWARD

"For great is your love, reaching to the heavens;
your faithfulness reaches to the skies."
—Psalm 57:10

Those of us who are Christians have a hard time not thinking of heaven as someplace "up." Jesus Christ "ascended," after all. Jacob saw a vision of a ladder descending, and Elijah departed for points upward.

That upward proclivity of ours results in part, I suppose, from some leftover Platonism in early Christian thought: the idea that this world is somehow less than sweet, that we've got to leave it behind like our old natures before we can ascend to something, well, heavenly.

There is, or so people tell me, nothing above us for miles and miles. *Nothing* is overstatement, of course. All sorts of planets and stars and whole solar systems are up there, so many that astronomers have never located a dead end sign.

But I have theologian friends who claim that the new heavens and the new earth really mean that "heaven" will be right here on earth. It's just that we'll have no more hog lots. Everything on terra firma will be lovely—a lá Garden of Eden. We won't be singing in some big choir; instead, we'll employ ourselves as we do now, maybe, only with no backaches or seat belts. Go ahead—create your own list!

I don't think David is being metaphorical here in Psalm 57, although he is using his official poetic license. I think he's talking about the sky, not some angelic heaven. The Old Testament patriarchs simply weren't as obsessed with heaven as we are. Last week I saw a pick-up with a license that said "TNKHVN" and I understood at least something about why they call those special order tags "vanity" plates.

I don't think David is talking about heaven, per se; he's settled on the greatest expanse of *infinity* his finiteness can locate—the skies. Saturday morning, the first clear Saturday in a month, I went out with my camera only to find the skies crystalline. A cold wind had swept away dust and fog, the sky was tin-foil bright and shiny.

Just as we need sin to make stories, camera bugs out here on the Plains need clouds to create a photograph, expansive as the skies are here. But then David is not toting a digital in Psalm 57. He's just praising the Lord, and what I'm thinking is that *this* sky—not a particularly good subject for photography—but *this* sky, the one where there is absolutely and blindingly nothing, is the one he's seeing or imagining, the sun not a disk but a huge burning smudge of colorless luminescence.

This kind of sky goes on forever—and now I'm making metaphors. This kind of sky is as limitless as David wants us to imagine.

But then, the literal subject matter of this line is not the sky but God's love, which David says, like Saturday's skies, simply can't be contained. In his ecstatic praise, he reaches for the only comparison he can imagine, and there's just nothing else anywhere under the sun more endless than a perfect crystalline sky.

In the end, even the sky—the limitless sky—is no match for God's love. The heavens, even when they appear to stretch out forever, can't compare. Nope. Like all of us when we have no words, David is doing the very best he can.

Someday we'll all have new vocabularies. I'm not sure where we'll be, but we'll have the words, at last, to make sense of what's now so immensely far beyond us.

<hr />

Lord, bless our anxiousness, our striving, our reach for language. Bless our day-to-day lives with glimpses of heaven, wherever that is. Help us live in anticipation of all of your love. Thank you for your Son, our gift. May our days bring your praise. Amen.